BATTLESHIP NELSON
The story of HMS Nelson

BATTLESHIP
NELSON
The story of HMS Nelson

Ronald Careless

ARMS AND ARMOUR PRESS

Published in 1985 by Arms and Armour Press Limited,
2–6 Hampstead High Street, London NW3 1QQ.

Distributed in the USA by Sterling Publishing Co. Inc.,
2 Park Avenue, New York, N.Y. 10016.

British Library Cataloguing in Publication Data:
Careless, Ronald
Battleship Nelson
1. Nelson (*Ship*) – History   I. Title
623.8′252′0941   VA458.N4

ISBN 0-85368-726-9

Designed by David Gibbons; map and diagram
by Anthony A. Evans; edited by Michael Boxall; typeset by
Typesetters (Birmingham) Limited; printed and bound by
Billing and Sons Ltd, Guildford, London and Worcester.

Contents

Foreword   9
Preface   11
Introduction   13

1. Flagship Home Fleet   15
2. Convoys and Club Runs   29
3. Force 'H' Again   65
4. Assault on Europe   95
5. Far East and Finale   125

Appendices:
I. Battle Honours and Naval
   Operations and Convoys in which
   H.M.S. *Nelson* took part   151
II. Admirals whose Flags were worn
    by H.M.S. *Nelson*   152
III. Captains of H.M.S. *Nelson*   153
Index   154

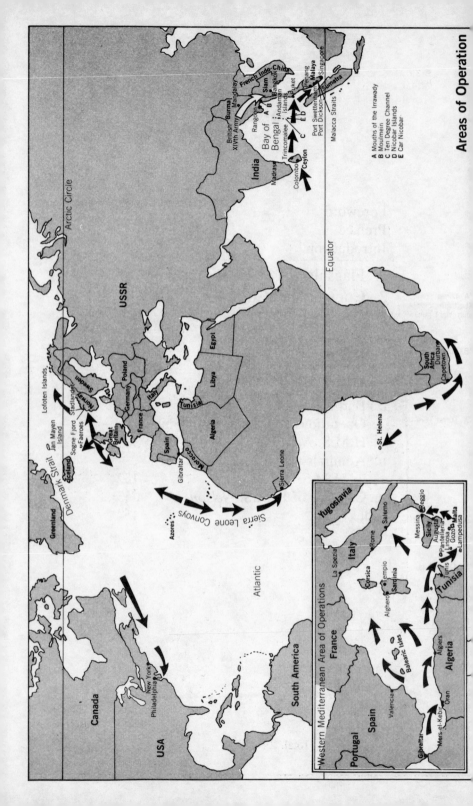

Areas of Operation

A Mouths of the Irrawady
B Moulmein
C Ten Degree Channel
D Nicobar Islands
E Car Nicobar

Western Mediterranean Area of Operations

Designation of the guns.

Main, secondary and tertiary armament. 16-inch, 6-inch and 4.7-inch HA.

Close-range armament. Octuple Poms-Poms, quadruple 40mm Bofors and 20mm Oerlikons

Port Side

Starboard Side

Oerlikon Groups

Inside the main armament turrets the individual guns were named Happy, Grumpy, Sneezy, Dopey, Sleepy, Bashful, Doc, Mickey and Minnie.

'A' Turret 16in (Left gun, centre gun, right gun)

'B' Turret 16in

'X' Turret 16in

'M1' Pom-Pom

'A' Group, 8 guns (Before 'A' turret)

'B' Group, 2 guns (Abreast 'B' turret)

'X' Group, 6 guns (Atop 'X' turret)

'42' Bofors (Port)

'41' Bofors (Stbd)

'O' Group, 13 guns (Octopoidal)

'HA2' 4.7in gun

'HA1' 4.7in gun

'HA4' 4.7in gun

'HA3' 4.7in gun

'M4' Pom-Pom (Port)

'M3' Pom-Pom (Stbd)

'W' Group, 16 guns (Waist)

'P1' Turret 6in (Left gun, right gun)

'44' Bofors (Port)

'43' Bofors (Stbd)

'S1' Turret 6in

'P2' Turret 6in

'S2' Turret 6in

'G' Group, 10 guns (Gallery to boat-deck)

'P3' Turret 6in

'M6' Pom-Pom (Port)

'S3' Turret 6in

'M' Group, 6 guns (Mainmast)

'M5' Pom-Pom (Stbd)

'HA6' 4.7in gun

'HA5' 4.7in gun

'Q' Group, 4 guns (Quarterdeck)

'M7' Pom-Pom

Total: 156 guns

Foreword

by Admiral of the Fleet The Lord Hill-Norton

GCB, KCB, CB

Ronald Careless has written a most readable and well-illustrated book about a famous ship, and done it well. It will have a wide appeal to old sailors like me, and to young ones too, as well as to the many men and women who enjoy a well-told story of the sea.

I feel I knew HMS *Nelson* well, for she went to sea the year before I went to Dartmouth, and I later served in her sister, HMS *Rodney*. They were enormously powerful ships in the days when the big-gun battleship was all-powerful. It is strange to reflect that they cost £7 million apiece – the Press, I remember well, dubbed them 'the seven-million pound mystery ships' – when today one would be lucky to build them for £1,000 million.

There are many sidelights here on war, and life at sea in warships, which are as true today as they were in HMS *Nelson*'s day. The danger of mines, which only her extraordinarily strong construction enabled her to survive at the outset of the war, is present today – and sadly neglected by the Western fleets, I am sorry to say. Life has to go on, even in the thick of war, and we read here about examinations for promotion, games and regattas and spelling-bees or quizzes, and sailors' jokes, because action is relatively infrequent, though alarming, and waiting for it is long and tedious.

Many officers, even some younger Flag Officers, will find it hard to recognize some of the words and ways which the author uses and describes, accurate though they are. They may find it even harder to comprehend the amount of sea-time put in, and the number of sea-miles steamed by these mighty vessels, compared with what they think is hard slogging today.

What no reader will fail to remark is the astoundingly high quality of the ship, surviving the most tremendous blows, and dishing them out too, and of the sheer professional excellence of the men who manned her; from the brilliant ship-handling by her Captains to the skill and endurance of the guns' crews and the stokers and the damage-control parties. They are a shining example to those who man our Fleet today, and though Her Majesty's ships are now small and flimsy in comparison, the people are just the same and just as good.

Above all it is quite clear that HMS *Nelson* was a happy ship, and there is no higher praise than that in any Navy.

Hill-Norton

Preface

For a long time I have felt that the story of the battleship *Nelson* should be told. She was the only British capital ship that was on active, operational service on the day the Second World War started, and was still on active, operational service when the Japanese surrendered six years later.

More important to those who served in her, she was a very happy ship. She had two or three nicknames, but the enduring one was simply 'Nellie', and undoubtedly it was for most people a term of affection.

Only when I retired from a busy professional life in the middle of 1982 could I contemplate this work of piecing together her history. By great good fortune I had come to know Captain George C. Blundell, CBE, RN (Retd) who served in *Nelson* from early 1941 until the end of 1943. He was her Commander during the stirring days when she was Flagship of Force H, the period of Malta convoys and the Allied landings in North Africa, Sicily and Italy culminating in the surrender of Italy which was signed on board.

I cannot exaggerate the debt which I owe to Captain and Mrs Blundell. They have been extremely kind to me and on a number of occasions have invited my wife Edna and me to their home. I have been privileged to borrow his private papers, and these have been invaluable sources of detail. If Captain Blundell should in some instances recognize his own style or turn of phrase it is because I could not possibly have improved upon them, and I console myself that he will forgive such blatant borrowing because *author's royalties from the sale of this book will go to a registered charity.*

11

I am extremely grateful for the assistance I have received from the Department of Photographs of the Imperial War Museum whose staff are invariably most helpful. To my wife I offer my thanks not only for her candid comments which have been most valuable, but also for her patience and forbearance when the work has taken up so much precious time.

Admiral of the Fleet The Lord Hill-Norton, kindly agreed to write the foreword, and for this I am deeply grateful. He is the President of the Sea Cadet Council*, and I hope that sales of this book may bring a useful addition to the funds of that splendid organization for young people.

Ronald F. Careless

---

*By the date of publication, Lord Hill-Norton, after seven years of service, had been succeeded in this appointment by Admiral of the Fleet Sir Henry Leach, GCB.

Introduction

The Flagship of the Third Battle Squadron was entering harbour. From her thrusting bow to the slowly turning radar gear at her mastheads she gave an impression of enormous power. Rising deck upon deck was her armament, one hundred and fifty-six guns bristling in all directions. Dominating them all were the 60-feet long barrels of the main armament, their mouths plugged now with the burnished tampions decorated with a profile head of Horatio Nelson. For this was the battleship *Nelson*.

On her upper deck long lines of men in tropical whites faced outboard. Above them, on the forward 16-inch gun turret, was the Royal Marine Band, and the strains of *The Standard of Saint George* floated over the still waters. In front of the control tower, a single rank of six buglers, dressed in the same tropical khaki of the Royal Marines, stood ready to sound the 'Alert' on their silver bugles, to bring the ship's company to attention as salutes were exchanged with other ships.

It was nearly four years since Singapore had seen a British battleship. Then, the *Prince of Wales*, with the battle-cruiser *Repulse*, had put to sea without air cover and had been destroyed. But now the last enemy had given up the fight, and for *Nelson* her long war was over.

On the admiral's bridge, high on the control tower, Vice-Admiral H. T. C. Walker looked down upon the panoply of his flagship. A spare figure, the left sleeve of his uniform shirt was pinned up at the elbow, for he had lost the forearm in the vicious assault on Zeebrugge. Close to him was the bulky form of Captain Abbott, his Chief of Staff. One deck below on the compass platform was the captain's bridge where Captain Clifford Caslon conned his ship in. A short stocky figure, he was a destroyer man at heart, highly respected by his ship's company. At his side was the commander, Commander Alexander Matheson, and a few feet away stood the navigator, Lieutenant-Commander G. G. Cowburn.

Charts of the area were a little suspect and the ship was moving cautiously. Although the echo sounder was on, the leadsmen had been told that their soundings would be more than usually important today. In the port chains was Leading Seaman Derek Davies, a most dependable man. With a regular rhythm, he heaved the lead forward and took his sounding as the hemp line came vertical, then coiled the rope and repeated the action. Each time the sounding was hailed to the bridge. Again he gave the rope the sudden jerk which sent the fourteen-pound lead whirling round in a circle to give it forward impetus before letting it go.

But this time the rope suddenly went slack. The leather becket joining the lead to the lead-line had parted. Many of the fallen in hands ducked, not knowing which way the heavy lead had gone, and there was a ripple of laughter. Fortunately, the leadsmen's job was almost done, the engines slowed, and a moment later the sea-boat was slipped and the boat-rope fell away from the guard rails in a long bight, towing the cutter forward until the coxswain judged the moment to let go.

Leading Seaman Davies was told to report to compass platform. As he entered, Captain Caslon turned and in a quiet, friendly voice said, 'I just want to compliment you on the accuracy of your soundings . . . It was very helpful.' The effect of his praise was short-lived. As the leading hand went down the ladder the Commissioned Boatswain, Mr Southcott, was waiting to reprimand him for the loss of ship's stores in the shape of one fourteen-pound lead.

All in all, she was very much a flagship.

1

Flagship Home Fleet

To the watchers on the Cornish coast, the ship doing her steaming trials over the Polperro Mile was unlike any ship they had seen before. Quite an ugly duckling in fact. Obviously she was a man o' war, but all her superstructure was crowded aft, and the only features of a very long fo'c's'le were the humps of her three heavy gun turrets. The date was 26 May 1927, and the verdict of the people on shore was to be repeated many times as the new battleship *Nelson* joined the fleet and came into the public eye.

The Navy thought that she and her sister ship *Rodney* looked like tankers or oilers, and because there was a class of fleet oilers whose names all ended in OL, they were soon called Nelsol and Rodnol. But in later years the ship was to command great affection: it was a strange reversal of those first impressions.

Nelson had her origin in the Admiralty G3 design of November 1921, which recommended a capital ship of 48,400 tons displacement mounting nine 16-inch guns, with belt armour of 12 to 14 inches, and developing 160,000 shaft horse-power to give 32 knots.

Also in November 1921, the Washington Conference to limit naval armaments began, and when it ended in February 1922, far-reaching decisions had been taken which included a treaty limit of 35,000 tons displacement for capital ships, and a ratio of naval strength between Great Britain, the USA and Japan of 5: 5: 3. The Anglo-Japanese Alliance was dissolved.

Thus the original, balanced concept could not be maintained. The Admiralty insisted upon the 16-inch gun, all the

15

evidence of the recent war dictated the need tor adequate armour protection, and, reluctantly, the Director of Naval Construction reduced the machinery to 45,000 SHP and the speed to 23 knots. She was to have a length of 710 feet overall and a beam of 106 feet. With the perspective of history, we now know that Britain was the only country which fully honoured the naval agreements of the interwar years.

In the same year the keel was laid down by Vickers-Armstrong at the Walker Yard, Newcastle-upon-Tyne, and the ship was launched by Dame Caroline Bridgeman, wife of the then First Lord of the Admiralty, on 3 September 1925.

During her power trials in May 1927, she recorded 23.55 knots, developing 46,031 SHP. On 9 August a navigating party from Portsmouth took the ship over from the builders at the Walker Yard. She had cost £7,504,055. She was brought up to full complement and commissioned at Portsmouth on 15 August by Captain S. J. Meyrick, RN, and she remained a Portsmouth manned ship throughout her life.

During the next few weeks her officers and men exercised her equipment and armament, and came to know some of her eccentricities. Steering proved difficult at slow speeds in shallow water, she was slow to answer the helm and had a tendency to turn into wind. But she had a small turning circle at full speed, less than seven hundred yards, and this was to prove extremely advantageous when she was under air attack. The new 16-inch guns had numerous teething troubles, and caused more blast damage than had been expected. Barrel life was disappointing and was substantially less than for the well-tried 15-inch gun. It had been intended to complete her with four octuple pom-pom mountings, but these were not available and eight singles were substituted, four on the conning tower platform abreast the bridge and four at the after end of the superstructure.

The huge box structure of the control tower was dubbed 'Queen Anne's Mansions', a reference to a section of the

16

Admiralty buildings in London. Another nickname which was given to *Nelson* and *Rodney* was 'the Cherry Tree Class', because they had been 'cut down by Washington'.

On Trafalgar Day, 21 October 1927, the flag of Vice-Admiral Sir Hubert Brand was hoisted and *Nelson* became the flagship of the Commander-in-Chief, Home Fleet. For the next fourteen years she continued in this role, wearing the flags of eight Admirals.

Until the war came her service was mainly in home waters, but she regularly went to Gibraltar for the annual spring cruise and for exercises with the Mediterranean Fleet, and she visited Malta a number of times. She cruised to the West Indies twice, on the first occasion proceeding through the Panama Canal; and she went to the Scandinavian ports of Copenhagen, Oslo and Stockholm.

Early experience led to modifications to the bridge structure during 1932–3, and in the following year two Mk. V eight-barrelled pom-pom mountings were fitted, port and starboard, close to the funnel, and in the same refit the torpedo range-finder towers were taken out. A year later multiple machine-guns were fitted at the after corners of the control tower. In 1937 extra horizontal armour was fitted on lower deck and platform deck, the high-angle control installation was improved, and a ship's side crane was fitted in the port waist.

During the summer months she showed herself at many seaside resorts. Little disturbed the even rhythm of life. In 1930, she played a part in the rescue of the master and twenty-two crew of the Greek ship *Fofo*. After an explosion in the merchantman's cargo of Welsh coal, the ship was abandoned and later sank. Ships of the Atlantic Fleet had picked up her SOS signals and it was *Nelson* that discovered the *Fofo*'s life-boats. A stoker who had been badly burned was treated in the sick bay.

An event which proved to be more newsworthy occurred in January 1934, when, as *Nelson* steamed slowly out of Portsmouth, she drifted to starboard away from the narrow channel and went aground on the shoal known as Hamilton Bank. A humorist at an Army unit ashore offered temporary membership of their mess. The press could not resist the Nelson-Hamilton connection and treated the story with varying degrees of ribaldry.

In 1935, she was selected for tests of the prototype 'Walrus' amphibian aircraft and, on 4 October, one of these machines landed on the flat calm water alongside her at Portland. Inexcusably, the pilot had left his wheels down and the impact damaged the aircraft's hull which immediately began to fill with water. To make matters worse, the Commander-in-Chief, Home Fleet, Admiral Sir Roger Backhouse, was a passenger, and there was a great scramble to escape from the after hatch. The only casualty was the observer, Lieutenant-Commander A. D. Torlesse, who suffered a broken nose. Ten years later, as Captain Torlesse, commanding the aircraft-carrier *Hunter*, he re-visited *Nelson* to witness the Japanese surrender of Penang.

As the 1930s drew to a close, the threat of war became more and more certain. In Britain there was a deeply-felt longing for peace, and the memories of 1914–18 were strong. Now it was happening all over again. German forces had taken possession of the Rhineland, Austria, the Sudetenland, Memel, and then the rest of Czecho-Slovakia, and were now threatening Poland, whose existence had been guaranteed by Britain and France. It was time to say 'Enough'.

The British Army and the Royal Air Force were small and in some areas ill-equipped, but the nation was fortunate to have radar and the new Spitfire and Hurricane fighter aircraft coming into service. At sea, the Royal Navy was still supreme, though not with the margin of superiority of earlier times. The Navy's greatest asset was its personnel. By 1939, all serving officers had been through one of the naval colleges; and the long-serving senior ratings were a splendid body of men who were to play a tremendous part in the expansion of the war-time Navy.

Britain possessed at that time twelve battleships: (two *Nelson* Class; five *Queen Elizabeth* Class and five *Royal Sovereign* Class from the First World War); and three battle-cruisers (*Repulse* and *Renown* from the war, and *Hood* built just after the war). Under contract were five new battleships of the *King George V* Class, but construction work was being delayed because of the vital need to devote dockyard resources to preparing new convoy escorts for sea.

At the declaration of war on 3 September 1939, *Nelson* was at Scapa Flow in company with *Rodney*, *Royal Sovereign*, *Royal Oak* and *Ramillies*.

The glass case containing the uniform worn by Lord Nelson at the Battle of Trafalgar, now in the National Maritime Museum at Greenwich, was sent ashore by drifter to Scrabster, and thence to the National Bank of Scotland at Thurso for safe-keeping. But throughout the war there remained a lock of Nelson's hair in a small picture-frame on the starboard side of the keyboard flat.

The brass gun tampions were removed and for most of the war the muzzles of the guns were covered with canvas bags. These gave sufficient protection against the weather and could be fired through if necessary.

General patrol duties occupied the first few weeks of the war, as German merchant ships attempted to return home and reports were received of enemy warships at sea. It is a popular misconception that battleships spent little time at sea. In the early part of the war, British battleships averaged only five days in harbour each month.

After the submarine *Spearfish* had suffered severe action damage while patrolling off Haustholm, the Commander-in-Chief, Admiral Sir Charles Forbes, took the fleet across the North Sea to escort her home. On 26 September *Nelson*, together with *Rodney*, the aircraft carrier *Ark Royal* and other covering forces, was one hundred and fifty miles off the coast of Norway when German aircraft launched the first of many attacks on her. The crew raced to their stations at the urgent call of the 'Alarm to Arms', and the crack of the

4.7s and the loud chatter of the close-range guns was heard in anger for the first time. The results proved instructive to both sides. The Germans inflicted no damage on *Nelson*, but in the flagship there was a dawning realisation that the six 4.7s and the handful of pom-poms and machine-guns were inadequate for A.A. defence. The Germans did, however, claim to have sunk the *Ark Royal*, a claim they repeated many times before it actually happened. They also claimed at about this time to have sunk HMS *Kestrel*, a Royal Naval Air Station on shore.

On 8 October 1939, *Nelson* sailed again with *Rodney* to try to intercept German forces reported to include the battle-cruiser *Gneisenau* and the cruiser *Köln*, north-east of the Shetlands. No contact was made, but the fleet continued to search until *Rodney* was ordered to the Clyde with rudder defects on the 29th. Instead of returning to Scapa, where the defences were not yet on a fully effective war footing, *Nelson* proceeded to a 'secret' base at Loch Ewe on the west coast of Scotland. It was not as secret as the Admiralty supposed, and the Germans quickly had a patrol line of submarines to intercept British ships.

At about 1000 on 30 October, Leutnant Wilhelm Zahn in *U56* sighted *Nelson*, *Rodney*, *Hood* and ten destroyers west of Orkney. He was in an excellent attacking position and from within the destroyer screen he fired three torpedoes at very short range at *Nelson*. Two, or possibly all three, of these torpedoes actually hit *Nelson*, but failed to explode. At this time the German Navy had so many dud torpedoes that the problem was affecting crew morale and eventually became a major scandal. The incident affected Leutnant Zahn so severely that for a time he had to be given a shore job.

Nelson arrived in Loch Ewe on 31 October and the First Lord of the Admiralty, Winston Churchill, and First Sea Lord, Admiral Sir Dudley Pound, came on board to discuss with the C in C the use of the main fleet bases at Scapa Flow, at Loch Ewe, and Rosyth. A decision was taken to return to

Scapa in the spring of 1940 when all defences would be secure.

On 21 November 1939, the battle-cruisers *Gneisenau* (Vice-Admiral Wilhelm Marschall) and *Scharnhorst*, and cruisers *Köln* and *Leipzig*, began a sweep to the north. Late in the afternoon of the 23rd they came upon the armed merchant cruiser *Rawalpindi*, on her patrol line between the Shetlands and Norway. It was a massacre rather than a battle. The merchant liner, armed only with a few obsolete guns, stood no chance and was quickly overwhelmed and sunk. Admiral Forbes sailed from the Clyde with *Nelson*, *Rodney*, a cruiser and seven destroyers, hoping to intercept the Germans, and his force patrolled west of Stadlandet headland from the 25th until the 29th. But they saw nothing of the enemy, and Admiral Marschall returned to Wilhelmshaven on the 27th.

Both sides were devoting energy and resources to mine warfare. The first German magnetic mine to be identified was detonated by a magnetic sweep on 20 October, and one was recovered intact at Shoeburyness on 23 November. This find was of immense value to the specialists in HMS *Vernon*, the Torpedo and Mining Establishment at Portsmouth, who very quickly hit upon the counter-measure of demagnetizing a ship by means of passing an electrical current through cable, called a degaussing girdle, round a ship's hull. Before this, however, *Nelson* returned to harbour just before midday on 4 December and as she entered Loch Ewe at thirteen knots she passed over a magnetic mine which had been laid by Leutnant Johannes Haberkost in *U31*.

Her hull activated the mine and the ship lifted and shook to the tremendous explosion. There were 73 casualties. No one was killed, but in the heads forward, many lavatory pans suddenly shattered and their occupants suffered lacerations. The ship's bottom was also torn in several places, mainly to starboard; outer bottom plating for a distance of 70 feet was forced inboard by about 4 feet, and flooding extended over a distance of 140 feet. There was shock damage to the ammunition supply machinery. Winston Churchill referred to her as 'our interesting invalid'.

Admiral Forbes transferred his flag to *Rodney* on 1 January 1940. Temporary repairs were carried out, a degaussing girdle was fitted, and minesweepers made sure that the anchorage and channel were safe before *Nelson* proceeded to sea on 4 January.

She arrived at Portsmouth on the 8th and major repairs began. The opportunity was taken to fit Type 279/281 radar and three more octuple pom-pom mountings, one on the quarterdeck and two abreast the mainmast where the after director control towers were removed. On 'B' and 'X' turrets four UP (Unrotated Projectile) mountings were installed. These were the brainchild of Professor Lindemann, the Government's scientific adviser, and were never successful. Less imaginative, but of great value, was the fitting of gun-shields to the open 4.7s, and of an armoured 'zareba' round the 4.7-inch gun-deck. Pre-war photographs show only guard-rails round this gun-deck; photographs taken in the first year of the war show a canvas dodger at the forward end to give a little protection. Even with these improvements, keeping a four-hour watch in northern waters was a cold and uncomfortable business.

As the events of the spring and summer of 1940 unfolded, Norway and Denmark were overrun by the Germans, and then it was the turn of Belgium, Holland and France. The threat of invasion and the voice of Winston Churchill stirred the heart of the nation. Even as the Army at home was being reorganized after Dunkirk, General Wavell's Army in the Western Desert was preparing to go on the offensive against the new enemy, Italy; the people were quietly confident and were thankful for a peerless Navy and for the small but efficient Royal Air Force.

When Holland was invaded, preparations to repel an invasion were rushed ahead all along the south coast, and on 6 June *Nelson* sailed to complete her refit on the Clyde. As she set course from Portsmouth, two minesweepers swept the channel ahead. It was a wise precaution for they exploded two magnetic mines laid in her path.

She completed repairs in September and left Scapa with the Home Fleet on the 6th for Operation 'DF'. Admiral Sir John Tovey had now succeeded Admiral Forbes as C in C. The object of the operation was to attack enemy shipping in the area between Sogne Fjord and the Grip Light off the Norwegian coast, which was beyond the range of aircraft operating from Hatston, the RAF's most northerly station, in the Orkneys. Planes from the carrier *Furious* sank one ship of about 2,000 tons, and a second ship was abandoned by her crew.

The rest of the year was spent in the fruitless searching for German heavy ships – a seemingly endless vigil for a nation exercising command of the sea and keeping the sea lanes open for her own use, against an enemy which chose its moments to send out small raiding units. In addressing his officers and men, Admiral Tovey referred to the task in the words: 'The battlefleet is the heart of the war effort.'

On 6 November, in company with *Rodney* and supporting ships, *Nelson* sailed from Scapa to search for the German *Admiral Scheer* in the Iceland–Faroes passage. She returned to Scapa on 13 November. Early in 1941 it was reported that the battle-cruisers *Scharnhorst* and *Gneisenau* were out, and proceeding north through the Great Belt on 23 January. The Home Fleet sailed at once but no enemy sighting was made. Shortly afterwards the battleship *Ramillies* reported a suspected enemy warship and again *Nelson* put to sea with a cruiser force from Scapa on 8 February. Again, the sea was empty and the search was called off on the 10th, although *Nelson* and the light cruiser *Arethusa* remained on patrol until the following day.

At 1700 on 11 February the ship returned to Scapa, and at 1945 Lieutenant-Commander George C. Blundell, OBE, RN (now Captain G. C. Blundell, CBE, RN, Retd) came on board to take up his new appointment as First Lieutenant and Torpedo Officer. He had seen action in the cruiser *Kent* in the Mediterranean, and on the death of the Commander had for some months been Acting Commander of *Kent*.

It is interesting to note his impressions when he joined the Home Fleet Flagship. Very quickly he warmed to the character of his new captain, Captain Miles, who, he found, left people to get on with their jobs with the result that 'there was no panicking' and 'the ship was as happy as the monastic conditions at Scapa allowed'. He was mildly amused by the number of personal 'cabooshes' (that is, spaces which individuals used for their own personal comfort or convenience) and when he questioned an ordinary seaman standing rounds outside the starboard 4.7-inch ready-use store, the young rating gravely told him that it was the 'Gunner's Mate's Study, Sir'. And when he heard broadcast the pipe, 'Fleet Gunnery Officer lay aft on the quarterdeck at the double', he really thought it was flagship stuff. For the next twenty-four hours he busied himself in learning the duties of Principal Control Officer and Air Defence Officer.

The following day, 14 February, *Nelson* was at sea for runs on the degaussing range and for sub-calibre firings. As a measure of economy, gunnery exercises could be carried out quite satisfactorily by fitting a tube of smaller bore inside the gun-barrels. At full calibre a 16-inch gun fired a shell weighing 2,461 pounds; with sub-calibre tube inserted the projectile weighed just 6 pounds. Similarly, sub-calibre firings by the 6-inch and 4.7-inch guns used projectiles of 3 pounds and 2 pounds.

On Monday, 17 February, there was a damage control exercise in the forenoon and the new First Lieutenant was not much impressed, but later in the day he spent two and a half hours going round the ship's electrical ring main (in those days the Torpedo Officer was also responsible for all electrical systems) and was struck by the immense strength of her structure below. Other exercises followed, and on 28 February the ship fired one of her 24.5-inch torpedoes in the Flow. The two underwater bow tubes were slightly angled to the fore and aft line, and fired a 5,628-pound torpedo to a range of 30,000 yards at 30 knots or 15,000 yards at 35 knots. An outfit of ten of these monsters was carried. Lieutenant-Commander Blundell summed-up his early impressions with the comment, 'Nelson is rather like a man with a great torso, huge knock-out fists and a pair of undersized, gammy legs.' Slow speed was a great disadvantage in a fleet flagship.

Sunday Divisions were cancelled on 2 March 1941, as the ship prepared for sea. Something important was in the wind, and Nelson and Rodney had previously been detailed to send demolition parties aboard two infantry landing ships. The flagship slipped at 1340, and proceeded to sea in company with King George V, the cruisers Edinburgh and Nigeria, and destroyers.

It was the start of Operation 'Claymore', the first British amphibious operation of the war against enemy territory, and the forerunner of increasingly ambitious landings by the growing Combined Operations Command which would eventually lead to the massive and complicated landings from North Africa to Normandy. The target was the Lofoten Islands, lying in the Vest Fjord in the approaches to Narvik, which with the rest of Norway had been overrun by the Germans in the summer of 1940. The enemy had quickly taken over the fish oil factories, to ensure that the valuable oil, essential to Germany, reached there in a steady flow.

The big ships provided the covering force. The actual job was done by Captain Clifford Caslon in the destroyer Somali which, with Bedouin, Eskimo, Tartar and Legion escorted the infantry landing ships Queen Emma and Princess Beatrix. The military force commander was Brigadier J. C. Haydon, with No 3 and No 4 Commandos, some Royal Engineers and a detachment of Norwegians.

The raiders entered Vest Fjord during the night of 3 March and surprise was so complete that navigational lights were burning in the area of the Lofotens as the force approached at 0300. Each ship had a Norwegian pilot, and timing and navigation were perfect. The landings were unopposed, No 3 Commando going ashore at Henningsvaer and Stamsund, and No 4 at Brettesnes and Svolvaer. Quickly the demolition teams blew up eleven factories and the storage tanks containing 800,000 gallons of oil. They also destroyed four ships, and two others were sunk by gunfire from the destroyers. The local Norwegian fishing fleet was at sea, and as they took in the situation they hoisted Norwegian flags and cheered and waved at the British ships.

Ashore, 225 German prisoners were taken. A total of 315 Norwegian volunteers asked to be taken back to Britain so that they could continue the struggle against Germany, and a few of these were women anxious to do nursing. A British officer asked by radio for permission to embark them and this was readily given. He described later how one girl came down to the landing-stage, but at the last moment her mother would not let her go. A little sadly, the girl gave him a handkerchief and a farewell kiss.

The troops had re-embarked by 1300 on 4 March and there was an uneventful return to Scapa where *Nelson* secured at 1430 on the 6th. The men of the demolition parties returned on board and the stories of their brief moment of excitement caused some envy among their shipmates.

There were more exercises at sea during the following week and gunnery results were encouraging. On Friday, 14 March, she sailed at 1830 with the cruiser *Nigeria* and destroyers to patrol off Iceland as there were reports that *Scharnhorst* and *Gneisenau* were again at sea, and also to cover Operation 'SN.69', minelaying between the Faroes and Iceland. On Sunday 16th she made a rendezvous with *Hood* and *Queen Elizabeth*, and on the 22nd reported a capsized ship in position 58°41′N, 08°15′W. There was no contact with the enemy.

A few days later the news spread that the battleship *Malaya* had been torpedoed abreast of 'A' boiler-room while convoying. Rumours were rife, and the principal buzz was that *Nelson* herself was to be detached for convoy duty, the flag to pass to one of the faster ships. With the German heavy ships at sea the Admiralty had the unenviable task of disposing the limited number of British capital ships so as to guard the convoys yet maintain a Home Fleet Battle Squadron of sufficient strength. As was so often the case the rumours were correct, Admiral Tovey was to transfer his flag to the new battleship, *King George V*. But first, for a short time, he had to use the *Queen Elizabeth* which had been thoroughly modernized, and he took his departure early on Monday, 24 March, at Scapa.

2

Convoys and Club Runs

Nelson slipped at 1100 on 24 March 1941, and proceeded south, entering the Minches at nightfall. The air was crisp and clear, and the Scottish coast was a lovely sight with snow-capped mountains well inland plainly visible. It was a light-hearted wardroom which decided that it was no bad thing that the Admiral's staff had gone because it was now possible to sit down in the ante-room.

At 0800 the following morning the ship was off Oronsay, where she joined one of the biggest troop convoys of the war. This was convoy WS7 (the code reference was popularly said to mean Winston Specials), numbering twenty-three ocean liners with a total tonnage of 484,147 tons. Commodore R. Elliott was in the *Empress of Canada*, and Vice-Commodore Errol Manners in the *Stirling Castle*. Formed up, the convoy was an awe-inspiring sight. Out ahead was the *Edinburgh*, wearing the flag of the 18th Cruiser Squadron, twelve destroyers formed the screen, and bringing up the rear was the old battleship *Revenge*.

Visibility worsened as the convoy moved out into the Atlantic on a mean course of 258°, and the chances of the ships being detected lessened as they became blanketed by cloud, mist and rain. The following day, 26 March, there was an immense, deep-chested Atlantic swell, and someone commented that it picked up the great ships like little children. An air alarm during the forenoon came to nothing.

On the 27th some of the destroyers departed leaving only the 6th Destroyer Flotilla. The following day at noon, the motor vessel *Georgic* with the *Revenge* left for Halifax, Nova Scotia. *Edinburgh* also departed the following day and on

29

Tuesday, 1 April, the destroyers *Duncan* and *Foxhound* joined from Freetown and two more, *Vidette* and *Wishart*, the day after.

The convoy arrived at Freetown on Friday, 4 April. The majority of the men in *Nelson* had not been to the tropics before and it was very evident that they were thrilled with everything they were seeing for the first time. They crowded the ship's side and great interest was shown in the natives who dived from their dugout canoes for coins thrown in the water. Everyone had a chance to go ashore during the week-end, although there was much work to be done and some of the Midshipmen had examinations on the Sunday.

At 1500 on Monday, 7 April, she sailed from Freetown and continued south with the convoy. The First Lieutenant had been asked to stage a Crossing the Line Ceremony, and there was so little time that it meant a period of furious activity for his organizing committee. On the 8th, 1,400 copies of the Summons to Neptune's Court were produced and the sailmaker was hard at work on the canvas bath which was finally rigged and filled at midnight.

The great day was Wednesday, 9 April, as the ship crossed the equator. The preliminaries were broadcast all over the ship and everyone heard the report, 'Line Right Ahead, Sir'. At 0840 the Court assembled in the recreation space and at 0900 went in procession to the fo'c's'le.

Considering how little time there had been for preparation, the dresses were marvellous creations. One Midshipman, as a maid of honour, looked so stunningly feminine that one of the officers was heard to say that he could hardly keep his hands off her. King Neptune appeared, played by Sergeant Moore, RM, and was truly magnificent, standing six feet seven inches and brandishing a 7-foot trident. By his side was Electrical Artificer Nelson as a comely Queen Amphitrite. The comic band was in front, and the bears providing traction for Neptune and his Queen on their chariot made from two 16-inch shell bogies, the attendants and maids of honour, followed by the court jester, the physicians, and the barbers carrying huge razors.

There was a cheerful noise as the band struck up, the bears took the strain on the drag ropes, but the chariot did not budge an inch as it was jammed against a deck bolt. This was sorted out with a lot of good-humoured banter, and then the procession moved aft to the waist, where Neptune descended from his chariot to inspect a guard of honour in most odd and wonderful rigs.

After exchanging greetings with the Captain, the investiture began. Fewer than one hundred and fifty of the crew had crossed the line before, and about one thousand three hundred were duly sentenced to the bath of brine and took their punishment cheerfully. It was a happy and successful day.

Next day was very windy with the convoy steaming at sixteen knots into the south-east trades. Good progress had been made, and without loss, but there was always the strain of constant vigilance and at any moment the heavy escort to the troopships might have to steam out of the convoy towards some smudge on the horizon. The Captain casually mentioned to one of his officers that he had been on the bridge for 32 of the last 36 days.

On Tuesday, 15 April, a concert party was held under the tail of 'B' turret. It is always remarkable how much talent a ship can produce on such occasions, and the ship's company laughed and applauded the various turns. Some of these were well-worn jokes but they never failed to draw hoots of laughter. One turn portrayed a Commander's requestman asking for compassionate leave because, as he put it, 'My wife's impregnable, Sir', at which the Master-at-Arms with a pitying glare said to the Commander, "e means she's stagnant, Sir'.

Early the next day the convoy divided. The cruiser *Newcastle*, which had joined on the 14th, took one group on to Durban, and *Nelson* put in to Cape Town, berthing alongside at 0800. There was a great sense of relief as permission was given for deadlights and scuttles to be opened, and fresh air and daylight entered the messes. The Prime Minister of South Africa, General Smuts, came on board on the 17th and gave an excellent speech from the top of 'X' turret: it featured a welcome to the British sailors, a little praise and exhortation, and a little bit of Cape history.

Nelson left the jetty at 0900 on Saturday, 19 April, and sailed from Table Bay at 1330. The scene was breathtaking as albatrosses, Cape petrels and myriads of other sea birds wheeled and swooped over the lines of ships of the convoy, with Table Mountain stark against a cloudless sky. The albatrosses and the flying fish proved to be a never-ending source of pleasure.

They reached Durban early the following Tuesday. A local pilot came on board and at 1130 he took her in towards the entrance but, being unfamiliar with the ship's wayward-ness at slow speeds, he took her in much too slowly, and half-way up the entrance she started to charge the stone groyne to starboard. The Captain immediately took over, but the ship was now swinging quickly to starboard, broadside on with the flood tide under her. To make matters worse the tugs were extraordinarily slow to appreciate the situation or do anything about it.

Just as it seemed that *Nelson* must run aground as she swung forty-five degrees across the channel, the bow tug awoke to the danger and, combined with the Captain's skilful use of the engines, the bow started to pay off to port. She eventually got straight and proceeded in to the graving dock where she had another tantrum and tried to charge the left-hand bastion of the dock. Captain Miles coaxed her into dock with just twelve inches to spare on either side. The bridge personnel were full of silent admiration for the Captain's ship handling, and noted particularly that through-out the incident he did not once raise his voice.

Soon, dockyard officials were conferring in the Captain's cabin as to what defects could be dealt with. Both watches were given forty-eight hours leave, and on Friday, 25 April, there was minor excitement when the Torpedo Officer was sent for to advise on a depth-charge accidentally dropped by a minesweeper which was berthed outside the dock.

Some used their leave to travel considerable distances, cadging lifts where they could. One officer had the marvellous luck to return in a Leopard Moth biplane which took him over Ladysmith and the Drakensberg Mountains, a wonderful, towering sight in the clear morning air. When he landed at Durban, he saw drawn up on the tarmac a reception party of senior Army officers with their red tabs, all immaculately turned out and canes under their left arms. Their faces were a picture as the plane disgorged merely a grinning Naval Officer. Ten minutes later the General they had been waiting for arrived.

On Friday, 2 May, a ship's dance was held in the drill hall of the Royal Durban Light Infantry. The organizing committee put a lot of effort into it, and beneath a canopy of paper streamers the ship's company entertained their guests until 0100 the following morning. It was a modest gesture of thanks for the many kindnesses shown by the local people.

During Saturday the dock was flooded up to about three-quarters full; at 0615 the following day it was flooded right up and at 0645 *Nelson* moved down the harbour and berthed at 'A' Wharf at the seaward or southern end of the Point. During the next few days the aircraft-carrier *Eagle* and the cruiser *Hawkins* came in. *Nelson* was to escort *Eagle* to Freetown and on Saturday, 10 May, *Eagle* slipped at 1300 and *Nelson* followed her to sea.

Durban had won the hearts of the sailors by the warmth of its hospitality. Many people lined the shore to watch them go, and saw the ships turn south for the Cape. *Eagle* flew off a patrol, and for everyone it was back to the strains of watchkeeping.

For two days the ships pitched and rolled in very heavy weather. They arrived off Cape Town at 1700 on 12 May, and just as they were getting under way the following morning at 0800, a big roller came over the bow and swept the cable party mercilessly before it. Like struggling ants

33

they were swept into the ship's side corners before No 1 breakwater. Twenty men were injured, five so badly that they had to be landed. Four more were swept overboard, and although lifebuoys and flotanets were thrown into the water and boats searched the area, the blacksmith and a leading torpedoman were not seen again.

Nelson returned to Table Bay to land the seriously injured, and left again as soon as she could to catch up with *Eagle*. Throughout the day, gannets had been all around the ships, unmistakable with their pointed tails, pointed wings and pointed heads, and the unusual 'flop' into the water when they took a fish. These Cape gannets have yellow heads and slate-blue bills. For the next three days the weather was sultry with the south-east trade following.

On the 16th the Captain decided that the ships should alter course to fuel at St Helena after dark. Judging by the numbers of ships being torpedoed off Freetown, there would seem to be several U-boats operating in the area and the Captain wanted as much fuel in hand as possible for anti-submarine work and maximum speed.

Next day, guns crews were exercised in main and secondary armament throw-off shoots at *Eagle*. In this drill the guns are ranged correctly, but are laid on a bearing with a precise distance correction. With accurate shooting the shells should fall as a perfect straddle of the target's line of advance. With a throw-short or throw-over shoot, the correct bearing is used and a precise correction is given to the range.

Early on Sunday, the 18th, *Eagle* flew off six aircraft to make a close search around the island. The efficiency and speed of operating the carrier's aircraft was a source of admiration in the battleship. St Helena was sighted in the haze at 1130 and by 1400 was well defined, a rugged, rectangular block of black land with steep sides. Lying off Jamestown were the liners *Queen of Bermuda* and *Rochester Castle*, and a Norwegian oiler which quickly filled up *Eagle*. The *Rochester Castle* was about to leave for the Cape and took *Nelson*'s mail, which was pretty big, an indication of the numbers of friendships which had bloomed during her short stay. At St Helena the 16-inch armament was kept closed up, and she secured so that she could slip her cable quickly in the event of any report of enemy surface ships.

At 2330 the force sailed for Freetown. There were continuous air patrols, and *Eagle* never failed to impress with the rate at which her planes took off and landed on. On Tuesday 20th, there was an upper deck concert, and in the evening a spelling-bee, Officers v. 'Hostilities Only' ratings. On the 21st, a Crossing the Line Ceremony for stragglers was held, with the Paymaster Commander acting as Judge. Some stoker petty officers had secretly organized a hose party and suddenly, in the middle of the ritual, five fire hoses were switched on and everyone was drenched. It was a great hoot for some, but others thought it just a little ill-timed.

A 'most immediate' cypher came through from Admiralty the following morning, reporting an enemy surface unit in the area of 9°N,25°W. At the time, *Nelson* was about 3°N,12°W, a long way off, but she was ordered to investigate. The Captain was concerned for *Eagle*'s endurance as she could stay in company for only two days, but throughout this and the following day she flew off continuous inner and outer anti-submarine patrols. To everyone's surprise, the search was called off on the 24th and the force was ordered to Freetown. White smoke was seen on the horizon during the afternoon and this turned out to be the destroyer *Boreas* which had been directed to pick up 61 survivors in boats from a Dutch ship. After tea there were boxing-matches on the upper deck. The contestants were mainly seamen boys, and as some of them had no idea how to use their fists the bouts were quite amusing. During the last dog watch there was a strong smell of oil fuel and the ship passed through the wreckage of a ship sunk the day before: bits and pieces of wood, even a baby's cot.

That evening came staggering news. The Captain came on to the bridge and solemnly announced, 'The *Hood*'s been sunk by the *Bismarck*.' Everyone knew that the *Bismarck* was out, having earlier had an enemy report from *Norfolk*. But the news was shattering, there were so many old friends in the *Hood*, and a typical reaction was, 'I can hardly believe that lovely ship is gone.'

Sunday, 25 May, was a clear morning of amazing visibility and cloud lighting, but all thoughts were on the drama being played out to the north. At 1030, the ship arrived at Freetown where a huge quantity of mail was waiting, and sailed again at 0600 the following morning, pounding north for Gibraltar at her best speed. During the day the semi-final of the deck hockey was held between the officers and the topmen. The officers won mainly through the splendid goal-keeping of Paymaster Sub-Lieutenant Marr. Masses of flying fish skimmed alongside as if encouraging the old girl to get another knot or so out of her turbines.

News came of the sighting of *Bismarck* by air reconnaissance, and of strikes by *Ark Royal*'s aircraft. Then at 1100 the following day, Tuesday 27th, it was announced that *Bismarck* was sunk. In the sinking of *Hood*, we had lost an old, well-loved ship, but the Germans had been thwarted in their principal aim to ravage the Atlantic supply routes and now their newest capital ship had been destroyed. The day's news also told of terrific fighting in the Crete operation, and of many ships sunk.

After the concentration of forces to checkmate the *Bismarck*, the Admiralty began to re-dispose its forces, and *Nelson* was diverted from Gibraltar to escort Convoy SL75, but shortly afterwards she was re-routed to Sierra Leone to pick up Convoy SL76. A few minutes later another signal made the ship alter course again for Gibraltar, the Admiralty adding apologetically, 'There is good reason for the frequent changes.' Someone suggested that their Lordships must have had a hell of a binge after the sinking of the *Bismarck*, but behind the humour was the grim realization that the dreadful situation in the Mediterranean must have created immense problems in the disposition of the fleet.

36

As the ship sailed north the wind and spray increased, but relay races were held on the upper deck on Thursday, 29 May, and on the 30th, the final of the deck hockey. The officers beat the stokers after extra time in a good, clean, exciting match.

The following day, *Nelson* intercepted the Greek ship *Mount Lycabettus* from Oporto. She was on the suspect list and had two Greek flags and two Swiss, with the word Switzerland painted on her side. She was ordered on to *Nelson*'s course of 025°, and was shepherded throughout the day and the night of 1/2 June until, during the following forenoon watch, contact was made with Convoy SL75, 22 merchant ships plodding along at six to seven knots. Guarding this convoy was the armed merchant cruiser *Cathay*, which was ordered by *Nelson* to put an armed guard on the *Mount Lycabettus* and take her into Gibraltar. *Nelson* stayed with the convoy, and a new day scheme was tried out in which the faster merchant ships zigzagged ahead and on the flanks while the slow ones kept a steady course in the middle. During the day, *Nelson* also tucked herself away inside the convoy, and at night she went six miles ahead zigzagging at fifteen knots. These frequent alterations of course were not occasioned solely by a need to adjust speed with other ships in the convoy; they were in any case advisable because an enemy submarine might be preparing a torpedo attack.

At 1400 on 4 June, *Nelson* increased speed to seventeen knots and left the convoy, signalling to the Commodore, 'We wish to express to you and all ships of the convoy our deep admiration of the way you stick to your arduous and dangerous task.' Back came the reply, 'Very many thanks. Your presence with us has been most comforting.' The relay race a few days earlier had been very successful and in the first dog watch seventeen teams each of nine runners gathered for another round-the-ship relay. Again, it was a most successful and spirited event.

While the race was in progress, the ship started to get DF

bearings and reports of enemy surface warships and merchantmen. At 1820 a ship was sighted on the starboard bow and full speed was ordered. The reports had been made by aircraft from *Victorious* which with the cruiser *Neptune* was proceeding south with another convoy. The suspicious ship allowed *Nelson* to close for a time, and then altered course away and increased speed. She was making about eighteen knots and the range seemed to close painfully slowly from an initial distance of 25,000 yards.

At 1830 *Nelson* went to Action Stations. No matter how many times one heard the bugle call 'Surface Action' it always had an emotional, spine-tingling effect, even in the early morning when, dragged from sleep back to reality, one knew it was only the 'Dawn Action Stations' exercise. At 1845 another ship was sighted on the starboard quarter and turned out to be *Neptune*. Fifteen minutes later the range was 23,000 yards and the stranger started to run out her boats. *Nelson* was careful not to follow in her wake in case of mines or torpedoes, and at 1925 when the range was about 19,000 yards, the quarry turned towards *Nelson* and hove to in position 43° 27'N, 24° 10'W. At 1932 a boat was seen in the water port side, and the falls were distinctly visible through glasses. By 1943, at 10,000 yards, two boats could be seen pulling away from her.

With a sudden boom and the whiff of cordite, *Nelson* fired a single 6-inch shell to the right of the German (for such she was) and ordered her to re-hoist her boats. And then again, two more warning rounds boomed out. *Neptune* was ordered to close and board. The enemy signalled her identity group as the Swedish *Kescholm* of 3,800 tons, speed 13½ knots, launched in 1937. But this ship was some 8,000 tons and obviously capable of about 18 knots. Nor did she have a Swedish flag painted on her side, though she was in typical Swedish colours of buff upperworks and medium-grey hull. She was a flush-decker with one squat, straight funnel, two masts, two very conspicuous samson posts forward of the bridge, and a big structure aft on the poop. At about 1950 there was a puff of white smoke at her side as a scuttling charge went off; *Nelson*'s torpedo-room crew below felt the shock-wave against the hull. *Neptune* closed and put a boarding-party in. Leaving the cruiser to deal with the situation *Nelson* continued on her northerly course. A signal picked up later from *Neptune* to *Victorious* said that the German *Gonzenheim* had sunk.

In the middle watch a cypher from the armed boarding-vessel *Marsdale* reported that she had stopped, boarded and captured the German supply ship *Gedenia*. So the network of supply vessels intended to succour the *Bismarck* was being mopped-up by the far-reaching arms of the Royal Navy.

As the ship entered the Western Approaches on Thursday, 5 June, she was joined by the destroyers *Electra*, *Imogen*, *Icarus* and *Antelope*. The semi-finals of the popular relay races were run: Quarterdeck 'A' Team, Accountants and Royal Marines, with the Marines winning; and Wardroom, Hostilities Only Ratings and Quarterdeck 'B', with the Wardroom winning. The weather was distinctly colder and everyone was wearing blues.

The ship's company had been hoping to see their families, but with the loss of the *Hood*, *Rodney* refitting in America, and *Prince of Wales* repairing action damage, leave for *Nelson* was out of the question and she secured at Scapa shortly after midnight on Sunday, 8 June. When daylight came, they saw that *King George V* was in; also the cruisers *Devonshire, Manchester* and *Nigeria*. It seemed strange to be back in that bleak place, with barrage balloons and air-raid warnings. The Commander-in-Chief was concerned that the Germans might try a spectacular reprisal for the sinking of *Bismarck*, and torpedo-net protection was ordered for the big ships. Many of the crew turned in that night with the pleasurable anticipation of their first night's unbroken sleep since leaving Durban on 10 May, but at midnight the alarm rattlers sounded because of an air raid and everyone closed-up. It was 0200 before the guns secured and those not on watch could turn-in.

On the 11th, *King George V* went out, and at 0300 the following morning *Nelson* was ordered to one hour's notice for sea and remained so for some days, though the reason never became clear. In the morning she shifted to the flagship berth so as to be in telephone contact with the shore.

The Captain was dined in the wardroom to mark his departure in two days' time, and in a fine speech the Commander told of a snatch of conversation between an officer and a look-out which went: 'The Captain will be missed'. 'Yes, Sir, any chance of the Commander going too?'

Captain Miles bade farewell on Saturday, 14 June, and in the afternoon Captain Tom Troubridge succeeded him. For the next few days the ship carried out a variety of exercises at sea and went through the degaussing range procedure. The news of Germany's invasion of Russia came through early on 22 June. Next day, the Reverend Harold Beardmore left for a fortnight's leave to visit *Hood* widows at Portsmouth. Of the crew of 1,415 only 3 survived. He had been the *Hood*'s chaplain and only missed her last voyage because he was doing welfare work among ship's company wives. The idea of sending him to Portsmouth had come from the Admiralty, and when one reflects upon the very great and momentous pressures upon people at the Admiralty at that time, one can only feel thankful that someone there gave thought to the bereaved women.

In the 1940s, to help new chaplains Harold Beardmore wrote a book called *The Waters of Uncertainty* which for more than twenty years was a naval book of reference. When peace came, he went to South Africa as Archdeacon of Basutoland, and his great spirit again drew people to him in commitment and affection as he became a familiar figure riding from place to place on an old horse. Finally, he was appointed Bishop of Saint Helena. He died in 1967.

At night there was no darkness now, and everyone felt a

bit naked when there were air raids. On 24 June, the middle watch was like a continuous serene sunset, very beautiful with the whole heavens tinted red, the ships silhouetted black, and the waters of the Flow opal and pearl. During the day there was a deck hockey match between the warrant officers and the 'veteran' officers (those over 35!).

Exercises continued, including a main armament shoot in the Pentland Firth; there were sporting events on shore; and on Sunday, 29 June, there was a march past by open list when each man saluted the Captain as he passed the dais. The ship sailed from Scapa to take part in Operation 'Substance' at 0815 on Friday, 11 July.

At Greenock the following morning there was hustle and bustle everywhere and a tremendous amount of shipping in the Clyde. There was *Royal Sovereign*, the aircraft-carriers *Furious* and *Argus* and a CAM ship (Catapult-Aircraft Merchantman), an MTB parent ship with six motor torpedo-boats athwartships on deck, and merchant ships everywhere. Captain Troubridge spoke to the ship's company at 1930. He said there were two things a Captain usually spoke about and which a ship's company wanted to hear. One was leave, the other action. Although, he said, he believed in taking as much leave as possible, he could not offer leave on this occasion. What they could expect was action . . . air action. The ship weighed anchor at 2000 and headed round the north of Ireland with the cruisers *Arethusa* and *Manchester*, destroyers and the body of merchantmen.

The Chaplain was back on board and the following day, Sunday, 13 July, preached a fine sermon on the subject of the coin shown to Christ. It was made of gold and a base metal mixed intimately together, he said, and the gold in us was the grace of God which we must always keep bright. He told how profoundly touched and ennobled he had felt by the spirit of the people of Portsmouth and especially by the courage of the bereaved *Hood* wives he had visited.

There were comings and goings during the next few days. Wednesday, 16 July, began very misty and at 1040 *Avila Star*

41

left the convoy for Trinidad. The next day *Pasteur* left escorted by *Manchester*, and *Leinster* with the *Arethusa*. Later the same day there was a rendezvous with the 8th Destroyer Flotilla and *Fearless* passed orders by line which revealed the nature of Operation 'Substance'. With *Renown* and *Ark Royal* of Force 'H', the ship was to escort a Malta convoy consisting of the merchantmen *Deucalion*, *Port Chalmers*, *Durham*, *Melbourne Star* and *Sydney Star*.

It was a wonderful evening as the fleet approached the Straits of Gibraltar, the sea white and cream with streaks of dark-blue and green, the ships black against the falling sun. Wonderful, too, were the flashing lights of Cape Spartel, Tarifa and others winking as in peace-time, contrasting with the Gibraltar peninsular which was in complete darkness.

At daylight the ships were well into the Mediterranean and the tops of the Sierra Nevada showed at an incredible height like a line of small, high, brilliantly white cumulus to the north. At 0800 the fleet oiler *Brown Ranger* came up to re-fuel the destroyers, and the cruiser *Manchester* joined. At 1030 the clocks went on an hour, and astern were the misty shapes of Force 'H' approaching at about twenty knots. At about this time came cypher news that *Leinster* on leaving Gibraltar in fog and mist had run aground on Carnheros Point, south of Algeciras and opposite Europa Point. A thousand troops embarked in her were got off and so avoided internment by Spain, but the grounding was a major setback and there seemed no doubt that the Spanish authorities would pass on the information to the enemy. From Vice-Admiral Sir James Somerville the order to the fleet was, 'The convoy must go through.'

Tuesday, 22 July, was a perfect Mediterranean day. Twenty miles ahead was Force 'H': *Renown*, *Ark Royal*, the cruiser *Hermione* and destroyers. The convoy was routed to pass through 37° 26'N, 3° 20'E; 37° 40'N, 6° 25'E; 37° 45'N, 10°E and at the last position, at the western end of the Skerki Channel, the big ships were to haul round and let the cruisers and destroyers take the convoy on the last leg to

Malta. During the day there were two air alarms but nothing materialized. In the forenoon watch on the 23rd the convoy was north of Galita Island when the alarm rattlers sounded and the well-drilled guns crews went to work. Men raced to their stations, and to shouts of, 'Start the motors', 'Close the bypass', and from the Air Defence Officer, 'Commence, Commence, Commence', a tremendous and deafening barrage was opened up on the approaching high-level and torpedo bombers. The sky was filled with bursting shells. It was a well-concerted attack, the torpedo planes splitting into two groups which came in on each bow and they were perfectly synchronized with the arrival overhead of the bombers.

Very quickly an Italian plane hit the water, and shortly afterwards one of our Fulmar fighters pancaked with a splash. *Nelson* and *Durham* turned towards a torpedo track which sped safely by, but *Manchester* did not seem to see it and a column of water shot up as it smashed into her side and the noise of the explosion became part of the general symphony of battle. She was ordered to hug the coast back to Gibraltar. This was another setback; she also carried seven hundred soldiers for the Malta garrison. *Hermione* was detached from Force 'H' to take her place in the escort through to Malta.

One of the destroyers, *Fearless*, was blazing aft and her oil fuel caught alight, sending up a huge, dense column of smoke. All efforts to contain the fire were useless, and shortly after her Captain abandoned ship, her magazines blew up. The Italians had lost four planes confirmed and two probables.

Other attacks developed later in the day, but were not so well organized and were broken up. As always, *Ark Royal*'s fighter aircraft did sterling work. At about 1700 *Nelson* left the convoy which completed its journey in the care of the cruisers *Edinburgh*, *Arethusa* and *Hermione*, the fast mine-layer *Manxman*, and destroyers. There was more firing at about 1800 and the destroyer *Foresight* picked up three

43

survivors from an Italian aircraft in the water. Throughout the night, the big ships steamed west at twenty knots while the convoy moved east. The Admiralty could not risk losing the *Ark Royal* in the confined waters between Sicily and North Africa. At 2200 there was a strong smell of oil fuel all around which persisted for some time: *Fearless* had sunk here. A cypher was received that the convoy had been bombed at about 1830. The only casualty was a near miss on *Firedrake* and she had been ordered back to Gibraltar.

At dawn on the 24th a cypher reported that the *Sydney Star* had been torpedoed at 0200 near Pantelleria by a motor torpedo-boat. She had seven feet of water in No 1 hold, twelve feet in No 2, and thirty feet in No 3, but the pumps had it under control and she was keeping up with the convoy. During the forenoon a shadowing aircraft was shot down, and at 1400 another attack developed, but the fighters did their job well and it was driven off. Later a cypher from Malta reported, 'Cruisers berthed. Convoy in swept channel.' The merchant ships delivered 70,000 tons of supplies and the Maltese gave them a great welcome.

A signal from Admiral Sir James Somerville, Commanding Force 'H', said that he would be transferring his flag from *Renown* to *Nelson* as soon as they returned to Gibraltar. Shortly before dawn the loom of a light was seen where there was no land, and a destroyer and one of *Ark Royal*'s aircraft sent to investigate found an Italian hospital ship searching the water for survivors from their lost aircraft. She was not disturbed. At 0820 there was the sad spectacle of seeing a Fulmar shot down by an Italian and dive at full speed into the sea. A second Fulmar got the Italian which managed to land on the water, and a destroyer rescued the crew. Radar picked up three groups of enemy aircraft coming in at 1055. The *Ark* had four fighters up and flew off six more, and they did their job so well that all that was seen of the enemy from *Nelson* was one group jettisoning their bombs on the destroyer *Maori* which received slight damage from a near miss. All day fighter patrols were aloft. As soon

44

as the last machine of a new patrol was flown off, the first of the homing flight flew on.

In the forenoon of Saturday, 26 July, the ship suddenly made an emergency turn away from a submarine contact report and immediately after a torpedo track was seen by *Hermione*. At 1640 the Force passed the *Hunt*-Class destroyer *Eridge* escorting the damaged *Firedrake* which had a great hole in the starboard side of her forward boiler-room. Despite her damage she was under her own power, making her way slowly to Gibraltar. Lower deck was cleared in *Nelson* and she gave three cheers as she passed *Firedrake*.

From the east, Gibraltar looked a perfectly marvellous sight in the morning sun, and the whole of the straits including the African mountains could be seen. *Nelson* entered harbour at about 1000 on Sunday, 27 July, and berthed at the south mole astern of *Renown*. Admiral Sir James Somerville and a staff of sixteen officers came on board, and his flag was broken out. On Monday, the 28th, a Board of Enquiry found that *Leinster* had made no allowance for drift, for westerly set or for distance travelled with engines stopped when leaving harbour on 21 July and in consequence she had run aground at 0349. Very different was the Board of Enquiry for *Manchester* the following day and there was no word of criticism for her officers: as the torpedo struck abreast 'X' turret port side, the main wireless office was flooded, killing everyone inside. Damage was widespread, but the fore and aft armoured bulkhead over the magazines and shell rooms had withstood the blow and this, combined with the exertions of her ship's company, had saved the situation.

Everyone had expected *Renown* to leave for home at once, but at Gibraltar there were still the 1,700 soldiers and airmen from *Leinster* and *Manchester* who were needed in Malta, and the fleet was ordered to sea the next day shortly after 0200. As the ships prepared to leave, a very thick fog came down, the Captain commenting to the bridge personnel that this sometimes happened as the cold Atlantic water met the warm Mediterranean water. *Ark Royal* got away at 0300 when the top of the Rock could still be seen, the great carrier a huge shadowy bulk in the thickening mist. But when it came *Renown*'s turn to go it had become too thick. Captain Troubridge went down to the fo'c's'le saying he would con the ship from there, but conditions worsened until 'A' turret could not be seen from the cable deck, a matter of only a few feet away. It started to clear at 0500 and *Renown* got under way followed by *Nelson*; it was still hazardous and at times only *Renown*'s topmast could be seen above a fog bank.

The operation was named 'Style' and was to be a diversionary operation by the fleet while the cruisers *Arethusa* and *Hermione* and the fast minelayer *Manxman*, with the destroyers *Lightning* and *Sikh* (Force 'X'), put out before dawn on Thursday, 31 July, to make a dash for Malta with the troops. Force 'H' was to go north of the Balearics to a point between Minorca and Sardinia, and destroyers and aircraft were to attack Alghero in north-west Sardinia. During the first watch as the Captain left the bridge to turn-in he said to the First Lieutenant in a sympathetic tone, 'We've had a long day, Torps.' In his role as Cable Officer, the First Lieutenant had in fact been on the cable deck from 0200 to 0700, had then done a normal day's work, and kept the afternoon watch at sea and now had the first watch ending at midnight.

At dawn on Thursday, Force 'H' was north of Ibiza. Sir James Somerville was in great form, sending off humorous signals and this was something rather new and different for *Nelson*'s signal deck. At 1700 the destroyers *Cossack* and *Maori* detached for the bombardment of Alghero; and at 0330 the following morning as the fleet was eighty miles west of Alghero, *Ark Royal* flew off nine Swordfish to take part in the attack. Force 'H' then steered 255° at twenty knots. Just after 0600 the planes came in, silhouetted against the dawn which was a lovely red with the deepest blue sea. One Swordfish fired a red Very light for an emergency landing, and immediately its wheels touched the flight deck there was an enormous flash of yellow flame fifty to sixty feet high, followed by a column of flame and dense black smoke in which the aircraft was totally enveloped for some minutes. The *Ark* eased down to lessen the wind. She reported that on landing a bomb had gone off killing the crew of three and two officers on deck. The explosion blew a hole in the flight deck about two feet wide which was repaired in about three-quarters of an hour, and then the remaining six Swordfish landed on in just four minutes, a splendid performance after such a tragedy.

Cossack and *Maori* were sighted at 0615 and rejoined. They reported setting on fire a large warehouse on shore, and the aircrews claimed several bomb hits on hangars at the airfield. Force 'X' arrived safely at Malta and left again the same night. Force 'H' steamed down the west of the Balearics and then turned east to join with Force 'X' off Galita Island, between Sardinia and Tunisia. All the ships returned from Malta, but *Hermione*'s bows were damaged from ramming an enemy submarine off Pantelleria. The entire fleet arrived at Gibraltar on Monday, 4 August, and the new flagship berthed at the south mole. *Nelson*'s crew considered it a dull operation: there had not been a single attack upon them.

A wonderful lot of mail arrived the following day, and everyone was noticeably happier. For some days there were exercises and storing ship. The ship's company marched past Admiral Somerville on Sunday, 10 August. They were getting used to his wit and unusual turn of phrase (when he spoke to the ship's company on the 7th he called the main armament the 'gas pipes'), and as Force 'H' put to sea for gunnery exercises on Friday, 15 August, he made one of his classic signals. The sea condition was such that the tug towing the cumbersome battle practice targets found them a bit unmanageable and did two involuntary turns. The Admiral signalled to her 'Steer east and stop skylarking.' Who could have felt offended by such a reproof?

Someone commented on the 16-inch firings: 'You feel as if the end of the world must have come. There doesn't seem to be much of a bang, but the whole world is filled with dazzling light, the bridge moves bodily, struck by some enormous force, and there's a vast tearing sound.' He might have added that, experienced from an exposed position, the hot blast was felt on one's cheeks even a hundred feet away and through the material of anti-flash gear, and one heard a strange sucking sound as the ship rolled away from the discharge and the sea fell away from her side. The Night Action Encounter exercises were exciting. This was a standard drill which had worked with devastating efficiency at the Battle of Cape Matapan. Having established a radar contact, the enemy was illuminated by starshell; as soon as the first starshell burst over the target the searchlights picked it up (either one's own or from destroyers) and then main and secondary armament opened fire. Done properly, it was a matter of a few seconds only from the first burst of starshell to the concentrated salvos or broadsides. On this occasion, the cruisers *Hermione* and *Encounter* acted as Italians, and it was a realistic and effective drill.

Operation 'Mincemeat' began on Thursday, 21 August, a minor side-show aimed at destroying the enemy's sources of cork. Force 'H' left Gibraltar at 2200 and went south of the Balearics. On Saturday, the air defence position spotted an unidentified aircraft, Flag A Sector F was hoisted, and two of *Ark Royal*'s planes investigated and shot down a Junkers 52 troop-carrier. Two Italian Cant planes also came snooping, but although hit they got away. The Force turned north between Minorca and Sardinia, and very early on the 24th ten Swordfish took off in darkness to incendiary-bomb the cork woods at Tempio, Sardinia. All the aircraft returned at 0630 and it was reported that the cork woods and a factory were well alight.

Later in the day there were reports of two enemy battleships, with four cruisers and thirteen destroyers, south of Sardinia. Force 'H' turned back at once, hoping to bring the Italians to battle, and a dusk striking force in *Ark Royal* was briefed. But the enemy refused to leave their own doorstep and, disappointed, Force 'H' turned again to the west, making up between Ibiza and Majorca. The attitude of Spain was always a cause for some concern – Germany had tried hard to persuade General Franco to enter the war against Britain – and at 1000 the following morning Admiral Somerville arrived off Valencia to give a demonstration and reminder of British strength, a formation of 30 Fulmars and Swordfish flying just off the coast. Someone maintained that because German radio had claimed to have sunk *Ark Royal*, the real purpose was to show the Spaniards that the old girl was still going strong. The carrier was immediately astern of the flagship, and *Nelson*'s bridge personnel were highly amused when they decided that the Fulmars ranged behind the barrier looked more like inquisitive cows staring over a farmyard gate.

Gibraltar was reached on Tuesday, 26 August, at 1430. The Admiral flew off to London, there was an examination board for able seamen qualifying for leading seamen, and the ship prepared for her next task. This started on Wednesday, 10 September, and its purpose was to supply Malta with fighter aircraft in an operation code-named 'Status II'. *Nelson* slipped at 2130 in company with *Ark Royal* and destroyers, and the following day was joined at 0800 by the carrier *Furious*, the cruiser *Hermione* and their destroyer escort. Ranged on deck, *Ark Royal* had 26 Royal Air Force Hurricanes and *Furious* 20. At a point five hundred miles from Malta, in position 38°N, 4°E, the Hurricanes would take off and Blenheim aircraft from Gibraltar were due to guide them on to Malta. The combined Force went east at sixteen knots. Friday the 12th was a beautiful morning, a red dawn, a flat sea and not a cloud, but no Blenheims appeared. They had not been able to get off their airfield because of fog at Gibraltar. Admiral Somerville postponed the operation for twenty-four hours and withdrew to the west.

49

The planned operation was followed exactly the next day. At 0530, *Furious* and her three destroyers positioned themselves five miles south of the main fleet; at 0630 the first three Blenheims arrived and *Ark Royal* and *Furious* started to fly off. Fourteen from the *Ark* got away safely, but in *Furious* the third plane to take off, piloted by Sergeant Findlay of the Royal Canadian Air Force, struck the island with his wing, the aircraft crashed into the sea, and he was lost. The remaining 23 Hurricanes of the 1st and 2nd flights formed up behind the Blenheims and flew off in the direction of Malta. Simultaneously, another four Blenheims arrived to escort the 3rd and 4th flights of 22 aircraft, twelve from *Ark Royal* and ten from *Furious*. They all landed safely at Luqa and Ta'Qali airfields, and the fleet returned to Gibraltar late on Sunday, 14 September.

After one day in harbour the flagship went out for gunnery practice, firing everything except the UP mountings, and arrived back at midnight. The following Saturday, an underwater explosion at 0740 turned out to be the result of a night attack on the harbour by Italian human torpedoes. Force 'H' ships were ordered to close all watertight doors and to raise steam with all despatch. The explosion heard was the detonation of a charge which had been attached to a merchantman, the *Denby Dale*. A hulk was sunk, and the *Durham*, only just patched up after her last Malta convoy, was also attacked. Dozens of patrol craft searched the harbour for any other signs of the enemy.

On Tuesday, 23 September, the *Prince of Wales* came into Gibraltar Bay at 2300 and her three destroyers were refuelled. At 0800 the next morning *Rodney* berthed and it was clear that something was on. Pulling races against *Ark Royal* had been scheduled for 1700 and the Commander said they must be brought forward to 1430. The First Lieutenant took part in the Torpedo Division cutter. Afterwards the Admiral demanded to know why he had not been invited to pull an oar!

There had been a strong rumour that the ship was going

home. The Admiral's flag was hauled down and at 1815 she proceeded with the band playing *Rolling Home*, heading west for the Atlantic. As Sir James's flag had come down, *Rodney* had hoisted a specially big and clean one. But Admiral Somerville was still aboard *Nelson* . . . so it was a ruse to try and fool the enemy consul in Algeciras. Moonset was just before 2130. A few minutes later *Nelson* turned round and was south of Europa Point again at midnight.

On the morning of Thursday, 25 September, Operation 'Halberd', Convoy WS11X to Malta, began in earnest. At 0800 the various forces met and sorted themselves out in position 36° 15′N, 3° 38′W. Group 1 was Force 'H', *Nelson*, *Ark Royal*, *Hermione* and six destroyers, which would go straight down the middle of the Mediterranean as if on a normal 'club run' to challenge the enemy, keeping well ahead of the others. Group 2 consisted of *Prince of Wales* (wearing the flag of Vice-Admiral Curteis), *Rodney*, the cruisers *Edinburgh*, *Euryalus*, *Kenya* and *Sheffield*, the rest of the destroyers, and the merchantmen *Clan MacDonald*, *Clan Ferguson*, *Ajax*, *City of Lincoln*, *City of Calcutta*, *Imperial Star*, *Dunedin Star*, *Rowallan Castle* and the fleet supply ship *Breconshire*. A total of 2,600 troops were embarked in the ships, which were all capable of at least fifteen knots. They were to take a more northerly course and both groups would meet on Day Three of the operation and proceed together to 10°E. All destroyers of Group 2 would refuel from *Brown Ranger* on day two. At 10°E all the cruisers and the destroyers of Group 1 were to take the convoy on to Malta where these destroyers would refuel. On the way, the cruiser *Hermione* would be detached to bombard the island of Pantelleria. Meanwhile the battle-squadron would operate to the south-west of Sardinia waiting for the returning warships and an empty outward convoy from Malta. There were high hopes that Italian heavy forces would try to intervene.

At dawn on Day Two, Friday 26th, Group 1 was between Majorca and Algiers. There was no sign of any other shipping all day, and only one snooping enemy aircraft was seen. In the evening, the Italian Admiral Iachino, took his battle-squadron to sea, the new *Littorio* and *Vittorio Veneto*, supported by five cruisers and fourteen destroyers.

Early on Day Three, the two British groups joined in one majestic array. All the eighteen destroyers were spread in a vast screen from 5,000 yards ahead, shielding the convoy and creating a large area for *Ark Royal* to operate her aircraft. She had eight fighters in the air constantly on patrol.

All was quiet until just after midday when intensive attacks by big, three-engined Italian Savoia SM 79 II torpedo bombers began on the convoy's port wing. A terrific curtain of gunfire went up from *Rodney, Prince of Wales*, the cruisers and destroyers. Numbers of torpedoes were dropped and some of the aircraft seemed to get between the battleships and the merchantmen, but they scored no hits and a number of the enemy were shot down. One machine, gradually losing height, glided right down along the line of destroyers and finally looked as if it was going to pancake right on top of one of them, but it fell into the water just ahead of it and sent up a huge sheaf of flame and a puff of white smoke as it struck the surface. It must have been an awe-inspiring sight from the destroyer.

From *Nelson*'s bridge all around were pock-marked skies, diving aircraft, the crack and chatter of the guns, and the enveloping gunsmoke. At 1300, at the height of the action, the Torpedo Officer suggested to the Captain that, as there seemed no immediate prospect of surface action with the Italian Fleet, the torpedo crews under the Gunner (T), Mr Harrison, should be withdrawn from their action station at the 24.5-inch tubes in the torpedo room and the torpedo body room. He wanted them instead to back up the damage control and electrical parties. The Captain agreed at once and the decision undoubtedly saved their lives.

Another determined attack was developing and a number of enemy torpedo planes were heading towards *Nelson*.

They came right over the screen, which seemed to have little deterrent effect, and pressed home their attack. The first torpedo to be dropped was clearly going to miss. The ship turned to starboard towards a second attacker, a Fiat BR 20, and it let go its torpedo when about twenty degrees off the starboard bow and some eight hundred yards away. There was no sign of a track and it had apparently run deep. To everyone's horror it suddenly appeared no more than 200 yards ahead and coming straight for the ship which was still swinging to starboard. The time was 1331. The torpedo track disappeared under the overhang of the bows to port. There was an interval in which people thought that by some miracle it had missed or run deep under the ship's bottom, and just as they began to breathe again there was a sickening underwater thud. The whole massive bow and fo'c's'le rose and quivered and the ship shook like a mighty animal in torment.

There was amazingly little splash. It was just as if a small sea had slopped over the side with a momentary, vibrant haze. Moments later another plane dropped its torpedo and again the ship turned to comb the track, this time success-fully and it passed harmlessly down the starboard side. This plane too came down the starboard side, so close that someone commented that he felt he could have knocked it down with his fist. But the gunners did their work and the plane came down into the sea. The ship was still making eighteen knots.

As the mighty chorus of barking 6-inch and 4.7s and the staccato close-range guns continued unabated, officers and senior rates went below to investigate the damage and to ginger-up the repair parties. With his wide responsibility as First Lieutenant, Torpedo and Electrical Officer, Lieutenant-Commander Blundell went along the main deck passage to the sick-bay flat and found all lights were out from there forward and below. The damage appeared to be below middle deck abreast No 60 bulkhead port side. He went quickly to the main switchboard and organized parties to rig as much emergency lighting as possible. At the switchboard he learned that all the dynamos had stayed on although Nos 1 and 2 had had a big overload for a short time, and the forward circuit-breakers had opened correctly and isolated the damage. So far so good.

Back at the centre of the damage, emergency leads were being run and he went down to the Communications mess-deck where he discovered water rushing in through a gash in the deck under the hammock netting port side aft, just forward of No 60 bulkhead. There was about two feet of water and through the hole he could see the glistening blue sea. He organized men to remove the hammocks, the lockers and mess stools and tables in the vicinity to give working space. After hammering the jagged edges of the hole to get it as flat as possible, it was stuffed with hammocks, tarpaulins were put on top, then sawn planks shored the whole thing down to form a big pudding. A party was organized to remove ditty-boxes and cap-boxes from the mess-deck to save the men's valuables.

The Torpedo Officer then inspected the quick-acting door to the torpedo body-room trunk and on opening it found the trunk was flooded. This meant that the torpedo body room was also flooded. Thank heaven the torpedomen were not there! He gave orders that the door in No 43 bulkhead was not to be opened as it appeared intact, the compartment beyond was probably dry, and there was no point in letting in water from the Communications mess-deck. He concluded that below the middle deck, the ship was flooded from Nos 43 to 80 bulkheads. The mess-deck abaft the Communications mess-deck had very little water in it although the forward stanchion (or supporting pillar) was buckled.

While all this work had been going on the enemy attacks had continued. One Fiat BR 20 was about to torpedo *Ark Royal* when it was caught in concentrated gunfire from *Nelson* and *Ark Royal* and simply exploded in mid-air. A dive-bomber was seen in its aiming dive, then it climbed and dived again but went on down into the sea. Regrettably, one of our own Fulmars flew into the fleet barrage and disintegrated.

At 1402 Admiral Somerville was informed that the Italian fleet was 70 miles to the north-east and closing at 20 knots. Sending his cruisers and six destroyers ahead, he formed his battle-line and altered course so as to position his three battleships firmly between the convoy and the enemy. *Ark Royal* prepared a striking force of torpedo bombers. But the damaged flagship could not maintain eighteen knots, and Somerville reluctantly ordered *Prince of Wales* and *Rodney* to chase the enemy while he took *Nelson* back to guard the convoy.

It is not clear whether Vice-Admiral Curteis was taking a leaf from Admiral Somerville's book of humour but he made the signal for 28 knots which caused some shocked amusement in *Rodney* as it was about five knots more than she had ever managed, even as a young lady. The *Prince of Wales* went ahead singly at speed and soon left *Rodney* far behind, so keen was everyone to bring the Italians to action.

Admiral Iachino heard that the British ships were coming, his resolution deserted him, and he turned away. When, however, highly optimistic reports reached him that three British cruisers and one battleship were sunk or damaged, he briefly turned again, but with sunset the Italians retired to the coast of Sardinia.

Nelson's speed had by now dropped to fourteen knots. During the dog watches, the *Ark Royal* and the three battleships turned about with their destroyers, leaving the convoy to go on through the Sicilian Channel. Men in the big ships felt badly about these partings; the vulnerable merchantmen being left with just the cruisers and destroyers to protect them on the hazardous last leg of the journey to Malta. Britain had few battleships and aircraft carriers and it was a fact of life that a capital ship was a capital target.

Some hours later gun flashes were seen at intervals to the east, there was a bright half moon, and just before midnight there came news that *Imperial Star* had been torpedoed in the engine-room, the destroyer *Heythrop* had taken some men off, and *Oribi* was trying to take her in tow. At the end of the day, the score in aircraft was eleven enemy bombers shot down; and three Fairey Fulmars had been lost, but two of the crews were safe.

Down below in *Nelson*, the pressing need was for more wood for shoring. Eventually, everywhere was supplied with electric light, enough wood was found and the engineers rigged up their 75-ton portable pumps and put suction down in the Communications mess-deck. A number of compartments came to look like a forest of planks with the amount of vertical shoring put up. Throughout the night work went on to restore normal electrical services. Big cables were run through the bulkhead terminals and were joined up to six-way boards and fed section boxes. A lesson of the action was that one cannot have too much emergency cable of all sizes.

The bow had gone down about six feet and the ship looked very peculiar from every angle. The flooding had many unfortunate results. All the food stores forward, the cold rooms for the meat, the flour store, No 3 main naval store (clothing and cordage), the officers' baggage store, and the torpedo body room were all flooded. On return to Gibraltar the ship was to have transferred its torpedoes to *Rodney*; the state they were in had yet to be discovered.

On Sunday, 28 September, the ship had taken in so much water that she was difficult on the rudder. There was much speculation about what was going to happen; after the buzz about going home for leave it now seemed certain that the ship would have to spend some weeks in dock at Gibraltar, assuming that with the flooding and increased draught forward the old lady would be able to get in through the entrance. At 2100 she departed for Gibraltar escorted by the destroyers *Duncan*, *Garland* and *Piorun* (Polish). The rest of the force stayed to the south-west of Sardinia to pick up the ships returning from Malta.

From the eastern Mediterranean, the Commander-in-

Chief, Admiral Cunningham, signalled 'Please accept a pat on the back to compensate for the smack in the belly with a wet fish.' Admiral Somerville replied, 'Thank you, but a kick below the belt doesn't mean much at my age.' In a report to the Admiralty, Somerville said that his Guardian Angel had been 'reprimanded and admonished . . .'

On Monday the 29th there were strenuous efforts to further improve the trim. All the heavy cable from the bower anchors was brought up from the cable lockers and dragged along the deck to stow it in the waist. A shackle of fifteen fathoms of cable weighed three and a quarter tons, and in all 32 shackles were manhandled aft. During the night the protective screen was increased to four destroyers and two corvettes. There was a great deal of anti-submarine activity and depth-charging as the ship neared Gibraltar. She berthed on the morning of the 30th at 1130, drawing 39½ feet forward and 32 feet aft.

Prince of Wales came in the following night, and *Rodney* and *Ark Royal* early on Wednesday, 1 October. Italian radio claimed to have sunk three British cruisers and four merchant ships, and to have damaged two battleships. The actual tally was one battleship damaged, one merchantman torpedoed and later sunk by our own forces, and one small bomb splinter hole in the stern of the Dutch destroyer *Isaac Sweers*.

Everyone turned-to in *Nelson*. All day de-ammunitioning went ahead and at 1945 the bower anchors were got out on to a lighter alongside. The Admiral's staff had been busy shifting gear to *Rodney*, and at 1830 Admiral Somerville came on board for a farewell drink. In a short speech, he said that, in discussing Operation 'Halberd' at the Admiralty, they had decided that the Italians would try to put up a better show against us after their poor performance on the last occasion, and the Admiralty were quite prepared to lose a battleship to achieve their objects of resupplying Malta and to intensify our attacks on the enemy supply routes to North Africa. He spoke of the debt owed to the

Royal Air Force for bombing enemy airfields the night before, except for Cagliari, and he thought it was the Cagliari boys who gave all the trouble.

On Thursday, 2 October, the ship slipped from the south mole at 1000 and went into No 1 dock. By 1400 she was on three rows of keel blocks, with no side shores. As the dock was drained the immensity of the damage was apparent – a hole about 40 feet by 20 feet, with the torpedo body room right in the middle. Lieutenant-Commander Blundell was able to enter the body room at 1700 and the sight was almost unbelievable. As the hit had been on the port side, he expected to see at least the starboard torpedoes still in their racks, but not one was in place and the wreckage was complete. Tails were torn off and engines smashed, warheads disintegrated, the torpedoes were at all angles, and one had been turned right round. The evident cause of so much chaos was that as the bodies of torpedoes were torn off in the explosion, the pipe from the air vessel was broken and the rush of escaping air at such a terrific pressure caused the torpedoes affected to whip round like scalded cats. He was silently thankful that he had thought of withdrawing the torpedo crews. No one could have lived in such a maelstrom.

Evidence of the force of the explosion was everywhere and it looked as if the enemy torpedo had penetrated first and then gone off. Bits of it were in the body room with part of the air vessel, and the tail-unit and propellers, incredibly stamped on the after thrust-race *in English*, 'Made in Italy'. The deck was covered with TNT from the damaged warheads, there were two holes in the starboard side of the ship caused by flying fragments; and an armoured manhole flying up from below had caused the flooding of the Communications mess-deck.

The work of clearing up continued on the following day. From the provision rooms the stench of rotting food was abominable, and cleaning them out was not a popular occupation. One by one the damaged torpedoes were got out on to the jetty; some were jammed and it took a number

58

of days and both muscle and ingenuity to extricate them all. The job was not finished until 13 October. Of the whole outfit only two torpedoes were serviceable and these were passed on to *Rodney*; the Admiral Superintendent of the Dockyard arranged that all the damaged ones should be sent back to Britain in the aircraft carrier *Argus*.

A blow of a different kind came on 8 October when it was announced that all letters from families at home dated between about 4 and 18 September had been sunk. The ship attracted a number of distinguished visitors and on 15 October HRH The Duke of Gloucester went down in the dock to inspect the damage. His presence at Gibraltar caused a particular problem for the Governor, Lord Gort. The Duke was to attend the garrison ritual of the Ceremony of the Keys, but which Regiment should be picked for this special honour? Lord Gort did not wish to appear to favour one Regiment over another. He solved his problem by asking HMS *Nelson*, and at 1800 on Wednesday, 15 October 1941, the Royal Navy for the first time in history performed the Ceremony of the Keys at Gibraltar. The ship was also busy in off duty hours producing a ship's concert, and the following day all the small ships in harbour were invited to attend a dress rehearsal.

The Trafalgar Night dinner on Tuesday, 21 October, was a very special occasion. The silver replica of Nelson's Column on the table was flood-lighted, and the guests included the Governor of Gibraltar and the Captains of ships and shore establishments there. Captain Troubridge, a direct descendant of one of Nelson's Captains, began his speech with: 'Your Excellency, gentlemen, we are assembled here tonight to celebrate an event memorable in British history and to the honour of the man whose illustrious name this great ship has the honour to bear . . .' As they dined, Cape Trafalgar was just a few miles away.

By Wednesday, 5 November, the hole in the ship's side was patched and everything was ready for flooding the dock. A story circulated round the ship that when, a day or two before, Sir James Somerville, who was already a KBE, had been awarded the KCB, Sir Andrew Cunningham signalled from the other end of the Mediterranean, 'Fancy twice a k(night) at your age!' *Rodney* had gone home and Sir James was now flying his flag in *Malaya*. He put to sea early on 9 November with *Ark Royal* and *Argus* to fly more planes to Malta. *Nelson* was almost ready to go: the torpedo body room was filled with 950 empty oil drums and bales of cork, partly freight and partly as buoyancy.

As *Malaya* and *Argus* came in on 13 November, the news spread that *Ark Royal* had been torpedoed. Next came a signal to report to Flag Officer, Force 'H', how many officers and men could be accommodated. The *Ark* had been hit at about 1615 by a single torpedo from an Italian submarine, she had listed heavily immediately and, abandoned except for a few key personnel, was taken in tow. At about 0600 the following morning she sank in sight of Gibraltar.

Only one man of the *Ark Royal*'s ship's company was lost. At first it was thought that eighteen men were missing. Some of these learned when they got ashore in Gibraltar that they were thought to have died, and one group was later seen singing in the streets a well-known music-hall song, *Ain't it grand to be bloomin' well dead*.

In all, 70 officers and 900 men from *Ark Royal* came on board. Admiral Somerville came to say good-bye on Sunday, 16 November, and at 2340 *Nelson* slipped her spring, took the tug's wire and then slipped her 6½-inch head-rope, silently passing *Malaya* and moving out through the north entrance. The cruiser *Hermione* raced past, a black shape with phosphorescent glow at stem and stern, and in Gibraltar Bay *Argus* formed up astern.

Just before midnight a ship was seen off the port bow, apparently a neutral, showing white and green lights. As she did not alter course, *Nelson* eventually made a course alteration, but the vessel came on, very close, on a converging course. It seemed unbelievable that she had not seen the British ships. A collision seemed inevitable, she was right alongside and coming in, but Captain Troubridge quietly ordered port fifteen to get his bow away and when her bridge was in line with 'X' turret he went hard-a-starboard and swung his stern clear. It seemed a matter of inches, and so far as anyone could judge, nobody in the other vessel even saw *Nelson*.

Spirits rose as Monday brought a long, gentle Atlantic swell. The ship was steering 282° at eighteen knots, with seven destroyers screening. At 1845 four of the destroyers departed, leaving *Gurkha*, *Sikh* and *Zulu* to complete the journey home. During the middle watch Admiralty signalled that a German supply ship was to the north of *Nelson*'s position. By now rough seas were sweeping right down the fo'c's'le and the weather continued to worsen, visibility was very bad, and there was no trace of the German supply ship. Things got steadily worse from Wednesday to Friday, when, at about 0130, two enormous seas came aboard and went green over the top of 'X' turret, higher than the turret, and swept forward. Water poured below in a number of places, through ventilators, and penetrated to the lower conning tower and to the switchboard where it put several breakers off. The emergency party was turned out when water got on top of the batteries in the low-power rooms and they gave off chlorine.

At about 0300 *Zulu* dropped a calcium flare, and *Nelson*'s officer of the watch pressed the buzzer for a lifebuoy to be dropped, but no one going overboard in such seas could have lived. West of Ireland the barometer was down to 974 millibars and at about 0500 it was ascertained that all three destroyers were hove to in the raging seas. *Nelson* went on alone without an escort. When daylight came on the 21st, it was seen that accommodation ladders were adrift and smashed, the starboard paravane holding clamps were broken right off and the paravane was jammed under 'A' turret, wash-deck lockers, bits of broken stanchions and vent trunking were washing about the deck. The Captain reduced speed and put the sea astern so that working parties could go forward and start clearing up. This also helped the clearing up below.

By the afternoon watch the weather had eased up, Coastal Command aircraft were overhead, and *Faulknor* (D8) joined with *Icarus* and *Norman*. *Nelson* entered the Minches during the first watch, and anchored at Scapa Flow at 1130 on Saturday, 22 November. It was blustery, misty, cheerless, and yet everyone was in good spirits and even Scapa seemed homely. She weighed again at 2130, leaving *Duke of York*, *Resolution* and *Renown* swinging in the Flow, and headed south for Rosyth at seventeen knots.

Homecoming brought a keener edge to the sensations. Everyone was elated as she steamed up the Firth of Forth, passing under the Forth Bridge as a train was passing over it, and went to No 14 buoy off Rosyth. For the next few days she de-ammunitioned, and at 1600 on Thursday, 27 November, the first leave party went ashore, about 750 men. Six tugs came for her next day, and at 1000 she was taken into the basin, through the lock, and under the big crane. Immediately, dockyard workmen were swarming all over her, the two high-angle directors were lifted out, and new radar gear, which looked as big as the top of a lighthouse, was being fitted on top of the mainmast tripod. Internal degaussing was installed, and the watertight arrangements much improved.

An invalid usually gets lots of visitors and *Nelson* was no exception. The duty staff were sometimes at their wits' end coping with the stream of visitors. On 4 December, some American officers came to look at the damage, then two British officers, and just at lunch-time the Admiral Superintendent of the Dockyard and his deputy arrived. In the afternoon there was a conference to go through the ship's A's and A's (Alterations and Additions) and Defect List, and the Dockyard indicated what they would be able to do. The rapid-flood compartments were all leaking and their repair would be the longest job, probably three months.

Throughout Britain, towns and cities were being encouraged to adopt and pay for a warship through increased national savings and the purchase of war bonds, and *Nelson* had been adopted by the City of Manchester. Edinburgh Warship Week began on Saturday, 6 December, and *Nelson* sent a Guard of Honour to take part in the ceremonies. Japan attacked Britain and America the following day, and hardly had this news been digested when the Navy was shocked by the loss of *Prince of Wales* and *Repulse* from Japanese air attack in the Gulf of Siam. The first leave party returned, and the rest of *Nelson*'s men went home.

As 1941 ended and 1942 began, Britain was at the nadir of her fortunes, assailed on every side; her Navy stretched beyond all normal limits of endurance with terrible, mounting losses in the Atlantic, on the Arctic Convoys, in the Mediterranean and the Far East. During the next few months there would be little but sacrifice and defeat in the East, and during these months *Nelson*'s scars would be healed as she prepared to re-enter the war.

3

Force 'H' Again

HMS *Nelson* slipped at 0600 on Tuesday, 21 April 1942, and steamed slowly down the Firth of Forth for the open sea. It was in many respects a time of new beginnings. She had a new Captain, Captain H. B. Jacomb, and there were many new faces in every department.

Her appearance was changed. The UP mountings (by common consent the 'useless projectile' mountings) had gone and on top of 'B' turret was an eight-barrel Mk. VI pom-pom. Thirteen single 20mm Oerlikons had been added, as well as pom-pom directors and barrage directors. The new equipment and the new men had now to be worked-up as part of the fighting team.

It was a lovely spring morning, but there was no time to appreciate nature's goodness. Everyone was trying to sort out a mass of defects. Many circuits were wrongly coupled, communications to the AA guns were dead, and the after master gyro was going the wrong way, and there were other headaches for various branches. It was late in the day when the ship arrived at Scapa Flow.

The next day, *King George V*, the aircraft carrier *Victorious*, cruiser *Kenya*, and the United States Ships *Washington*, *Wasp*, *Tuscaloosa* and *Wichita* went out on Russian convoy duty.

At 0500 on Thursday 30th, the ship prepared for sea. The guns needed all the training they could get, and mock attacks carried out by RAF Beauforts and dive-bombers were excellent. After a very valuable day the ship returned in foul weather and secured to the buoy with great difficulty, the picket-boat breaking its funnel on the anchor hanging

65

from the cathead. After the long day's exercises this was not the humorous incident it might otherwise have been; it was just maddening.

In calm weather, coming to a buoy was a straightforward exercise. So that the anchor chain could be shackled to the buoy, it was necessary to remove the anchor; and while the ship was still at sea the work began of passing a wire rope round the centre-line capstan, through a fitting on the ship's side called a cathead, and then outboard to the hawse-pipe where it was shackled to the ring of the anchor. As the cable-holder veered or paid out on the anchor cable, the capstan hauled in on the wire rope and the anchor was lowered from the hawse-pipe and drawn to the cathead, where it was secured. The chain cable attached to the ring of the anchor could then be 'broken', and the cable was free to be used at the buoy.

Simultaneously, the sea-boat was manned and as the ship approached the buoy, the boat was lowered and slipped. It was then towed through the water by a rope attached well forward in the ship, and the boat's coxswain let go this boat-rope when his crew were all ready, with their oars out, and he was near enough to the buoy. A few strokes took him to the buoy and a rating known as the 'buoy-jumper' clambered out on to the buoy. The Captain nosed the ship up to the buoy and the buoy-jumper grabbed hold of a picking-up rope which was passed down the hawse-pipe. At the end of it was a spring clip very much like the end of a dog's lead, and this he clipped on to the ring of the buoy. Once the picking-up rope was on, the chain cable was lowered and finally shackled to the ring of the buoy.

In bad weather the whole operation could be a nightmare. There was sometimes a danger of the sea-boat being crushed between a large, heavy buoy and the bows of the ship. Or, as in this instance, the sea might be so rough that a sea-boat could not be used and the buoy-jumper had to jump from a large power-boat (or, occasionally, even from a motor fishing vessel sent out specially from the shore).

The following Monday, *King George V* came in with a shattered bow from ramming the destroyer *Punjabi*, whose depth-charges went off as she sank. It was a lamentable accident. Next day, *Nelson* was out again for exercises in the Pentland Firth, returning at 2300. Dockyard workers arrived on 6 May to help with the long list of 'not dones', mainly unpacked glands and unsecured cable guards. At 1530 Vice-Admiral Curteis arrived and his flag was broken out, but he remained only a few days and then left for *Malaya* and a Malta convoy.

The days were flying and there was no time to be bored. There were more exercises, including listing the ship ten degrees in a damage control exercise, and although it seemed an amazing angle at first, everyone soon got used to it.

On Wednesday, 27 May, the ship went into the Pentlands for more exercises and in the evening she headed west and then turned south through the Minches. At Greenock the next day the banks of the Clyde looked quite beautiful. The trees were in their new leaves, the different greens contrasting one with another.

Nelson took on stores. On Sunday, 31 May, about 600 personnel joined, mainly Royal Air Force, who said they were going to Lagos. At 2300 the ship weighed anchor and the following morning at 0500 the Liverpool and Clyde portions of the convoy formed up. There were 24 large merchantmen in all. With *Nelson* to escort them was the aircraft carrier *Argus* and ten destroyers.

During the first watch visibility worsened. The destroyer leader *Keppel* gave a 'Submarine in Sight' report, and shortly after it was thought that one of the convoy had given the six-blast distress signal. Fog came down thickly, Second Degree Damage Control was ordered, a fog buoy was streamed (this was a special buoy towed aft at a set distance, and the next ship astern kept it just off her bow), and extra look-outs were put forward. In this very poor visibility, a ship seemed to charge across the port bow and the Captain

67

went slow both, but there was no time to let *Argus* know and she came roaring up, just missed *Nelson*, sheered off to port and herself came up against the ship which had tried to cross ahead. *Argus* steered over to starboard and missed *Nelson* by feet only. Many seasoned men said it was the nearest thing they had seen, the carrier coming out of the mist with figures running forward on the flight deck. It remained thick throughout the night.

On 2 June it was evident that no ship had been hit during the night. The convoy regained accurate station-keeping and when darkness came thick fog returned. The great thing was to keep going on the same course and speed. When enveloped by fog the tendency was to close in on the centre, but if a ship appeared it was always possible to pull out a degree or so before there was a danger of a collision.

At 0100 on 5 June, the Type 273 radar reported an echo on Red 40 nine miles distant. If it was a submarine it was in a good attacking position; if a merchant ship it was likely to foul the convoy. The 273 report was quite definite and when a smaller blip showed up near the first blip the Captain was called. By now such armament as was closed up was trained on the bearing and ready. The 284 radar was also brought in. It was known that an enemy supply ship was out. The Captain ordered 'Action Stations', the rattlers sounded, and the ship's company were splendid in closing-up at their posts quickly. The RAF passengers were a bit bewildered by it all. An emergency turn of forty-five degrees to port was ordered by the Commodore and radar then tracked the 'enemy' down the starboard side and the destroyer *Derwent* was told to investigate. Meanwhile *Nelson* sighted a ship on the port bow, challenged and fired starshell and ordered *Burnham* to investigate. As the starshell burst overhead it revealed the *New Zealand Star*, very badly out of her convoy station. Then on the starboard quarter *Derwent* fired starshell. Caught in the brilliant phosphorescent light were two armed trawlers escorting a British tanker. So they too were friendly, but very far from their assumed position. Leaving

68

the duty watch, everyone went back to bed.

The convoy passed the Azores on 6 June. The next day the liner *Aquitania* went on alone at nineteen knots, passing between *Nelson* and the Commodore and giving three cheers as she passed. The destroyers took it in turns to come alongside for fuel and fresh bread. On 10 June it was learned that *Rodney* and three destroyers were not far behind.

A tragedy occurred on Saturday 13 June. Alongside 'A' turret on the upper deck were three long wooden booms each side, stowed in crutches. When the ship was at anchor or at a buoy, one each side was fitted at right angles to the ship's side and, from the boat ropes and ladders hanging from them, the ship's boats lay snugly alongside. The other four could be set up as ammunition derricks. Each was about twelve inches in diameter, and the hollow between any two was surprisingly comfortable for a man lying down. Just after 0400 Stoker Blades came up from the middle watch, lay down on the booms, and fell fast alseep. At about 0420 'A' turret trained round on a bearing on the starboard bow, the rear of the turret silently swung over the booms with a clearance of about four inches, and Stoker Blades was crushed to death.

At 'Dawn Action Stations' he was found. He was taken to the sick-bay bathroom and there sewn up in his hammock. At 0900 a sad procession moved aft to the quarterdeck, the Chaplain read a short funeral service, the Guard fired a salute and 'Last Post' was sounded, and the body of the unfortunate stoker was committed to the sea. At 1130 the convoy arrived at Freetown and *Nelson* anchored off Government Wharf.

More ships came in, including some American, and *Rodney* arrived on the 15th. At 1100 on Friday, 19 June, the convoy proceeded to sea and more exercises began. On the 21st there were many emergency turns. When a destroyer made a contact she hoisted a black pendant and the Commodore on seeing this blew a long blast of four to six seconds and hoisted international Flag E (or I) which signified 'Stand by for emergency turn of 45° to Starboard (or Port).' When every ship in the convoy had acknowledged, the Commodore hauled down his signal and the order was executed. This convoy was wonderfully good and it was a fine sight to see them all altering as one on to a new course, sometimes with two emergency turns in succession so that the convoy quickly moved at ninety degrees to its original course. For normal alterations of course the convoy wheeled round instead of turning, usually not more than twenty degrees at a time.

At supper time on the 21st the preliminary dialogue for another Crossing the Line Ceremony was broadcast as the ship neared the equator. At 0900 the next day the ship piped down and Neptune and his court assembled abaft No 1 breakwater. The routine was much the same as in 1941, but this time the part of Neptune was played by the Commander, Commander Hill, who stood six feet two inches, and Amphitrite by the Chief Bosun's Mate, Chief Petty Officer Sadler, who was about five feet. Able Seaman Yorke was dressed as a jester, wearing a red cap and a green suit, and holding as his toy balloon a big meteorological balloon; with his figure he seemed to have stepped straight out of the sixteenth century. One man had a cardboard top hat surmounted by model aerials of Type 279 radar, and the Chief of Police had 'Gestapo' written on his.

On this occasion the bath of brine had been made bigger and broader, but with the roll of the ship this had the disadvantage that the water swished violently from one side to the other and eventually the bath-side broke. The court adjourned while repairs were undertaken. At the end of the day it was all voted a great success.

The convoy maintained a steady nineteen knots, and was never more than 600 miles from the land all the way to the Cape. At 1140 on Friday, 26 June, *Nelson* and *Rodney* left the convoy as it reached 12° S. The two ships went ahead, turned and came down through the lines of ships, cheering ship. The Commodore made the signal: 'We thank you for your protection and our safety. Your many friends will follow your progress in full confidence that when the opportunity offers you and your gallant ships' companies will add fresh lustre to the honoured names that you bear. Good-bye. Good luck. God speed.'

On the way back to Freetown, as many exercises as possible were crammed in, and the new radar was a great success, especially in the Night Action Encounter drills. There was great interest in the 6-inch AA firings by the new barrage directors. The two battleships used each other as targets for 16-inch throw-off shoots; and with her new radar *Nelson* also did a blind 16-inch shoot.

At 1800 on Tuesday, 30 June, Lieutenant-Commander Blundell was in his cabin when a messenger came in with a signal from the Captain, 'Heartiest Congratulations.' Now it was one of Captain Jacomb's polite, humorous little habits that if something went wrong in the ship's routine, he would send a 'Congratulations' note to the Head of Department, which meant that he wished to discuss it. George Blundell tried to think what it might be. There had been two misfires in the day's shoot, and perhaps the Captain thought they were electrical failures.

Then another signal came. It was the time of the half-yearly promotions. He had been promoted to Commander. So that was it! And Commander Hill was promoted to Captain. Then kind messages arrived from the Warrant Officers' Mess and from the Gunroom.

The ships anchored at Freetown at 1500 on 1 July in a heavy rainstorm. A few days later *Malaya* left with Convoy WS20.

During the afternoon of 6 July, Commander Blundell was told that the Captain wished to see him. He found him pacing his cabin smiling broadly, and he seemed to be bursting with something. 'You remember you came and asked me to write about your next job,' the Captain said, 'Well, it all seems to have settled itself.' He handed over a yellow cypher message to this effect: 'Lt. Cdr. Gretton will leave U.K. 11 July to relieve Blundell. On relief Blundell to relieve Hill as Commander of *Nelson*. On relief Hill to fly home to take up important appointment. Blundell to remain at least one year in *Nelson* to prevent dislocation of fighting efficiency.'

Commander Blundell was dumbfounded. It was unusual for an officer to remain in the same ship on promotion, and here he had been given one of the plum jobs in the Navy, Commander of *Nelson*.

As people unused to the Navy sometimes speak of the Captain of a ship as its Commander, a few words of explanation may be helpful. With ships of all sizes it is usual to refer to the officer in command, whatever his rank, as the Captain. In smaller war vessels his next senior officer is the First Lieutenant, who is responsible for the day to day running of the ship in the execution of the Captain's policies. But in the largest vessels, battleships, aircraft carriers and cruisers, the extent of those responsibilities required a further senior appointment between the Captain and First Lieutenant, that of Commander. In a battleship, the Captain was of Captain's rank, the Commander of Commander's rank, and the First Lieutenant, who as a general rule was Cable Officer, was the senior Lieutenant-Commander.

The following day came news that the ship was again to be Flagship of Force 'H', and that Somerville was being relieved as Flag Officer, Force 'H', by Rear-Admiral E. N. Syfret. The Admiral's staff joined on the 9th.

At 'hands fall-in' on Friday, 10 July, it was found that the 2nd motor-boat had sunk and there was just a foot of her stern showing above water. The strong Freetown current made things difficult, but she was got under the main derrick and by using boats' gripes (the bands of plaited rope covered with canvas which held a boat in tight at the davits) she was turned on her side and then gradually righted, her own slings were put on, and she was hoisted bit by bit, pumping out with a 75-ton pump from deck level. The cause of the sinking was found to be a broken exhaust pipe and consequent flooding through the exhaust hole in the stern.

At an early stage the new Commander came to two decisions. The first was that in action he would remain in one spot so that everyone would know where to find him. His experience in the cruiser *Kent*, when she was heavily battered off Bardia, had created an indelible impression: there had been a period of confusion when officers and men had needed leadership, the Commander had been killed, and Commander Blundell had then taken over as Acting Commander at the height of the action. He now decided that he and the Engineer Commander would always be in the upper conning tower in action. By this means, with the Captain fighting the ship from the bridge and the Commander in the UCT, the ship would never be leaderless and if she were damaged the various Heads of Departments would always be able to get in touch with him.

The second decision arose out of the sinking of the *Ark Royal*. Commander Blundell had always felt that there was something badly wrong when a big ship foundered after being hit by a single torpedo. With the Chief, he spent many long hours poring over the ship's drawings and assuming that she had been hit in different places all round her hull. For each situation they formulated the best damage control measure to save her. Maintaining the trim was the answer; quick action with counter-flooding to maintain the trim. When the Commander and Chief Engineer had finished their calculations, they decided that, with the right decisions, *Nelson* could take in 56,000 tons of water and they could still save her, so long as she was kept on an even keel. It was an amazing conclusion.

Late on Monday, 13 July, a signal from Admiralty notified the promotion of Syfret to Vice-Admiral. This was just too much for the 1st motor-boat (which was designated as his temporary barge) for when all boats were called away the following morning she left the ship's side and then blew up. In the petrol vapour explosion, for such it was, the sternsheetman and the after canopy were blown overboard and a fire started aft. The Midshipman dived in after the sternsheetman and the rest of the crew followed suit; so that the picket-boat going to put out the fire had instead to pick up the men in the water. *Rodney* and the cruiser *Danae* were asked to provide boat assistance, but the fire got a big hold and she burnt out aft while the 3rd motor-boat towed her inshore off Carr's Point. Coming so soon after the damage to the 2nd motor-boat this was a very serious blow and temporarily left the ship with only two power-boats in use.

The ship prepared for sea, awnings were stowed, and she sailed at 0630 on Friday, 17 July, with *Rodney* and the destroyers *Pathfinder* and *Derwent*. At 1700 emergency procedure was exercised, by piping first the 'Still' and after a moment 'All damage control parties close up. Emergency procedure in force.' Then followed for the rest of the ship's company one of a number of alternative orders: 'Action Stations', 'Alarm to Arms' for an air attack, or simply the order to fall in by Division or Watch on the upper deck (by day) or main deck (by night).

During the night there were numerous warnings of enemy submarines and the force made many course alterations. When daylight came the impressive lines of a convoy were close at hand.

Sunday, 19 July, was a National Day of Prayer for the Royal Navy and the Merchant Navy, and Divisions were held on the upper deck.

In the early hours of the 20th *Pathfinder* surprised a U-boat on the surface and tried to ram. She just missed and as she passed only a few yards away, the submarine's diving klaxon was heard quite distinctly. *Pathfinder* whipped round to attack the German with depth-charges. Simultaneously, starshells were seen well to starboard as a Sierra Leone convoy came under submarine attack. It looked as if a line of U-boats stretched from the Cape Verde Islands to the mainland. There was no conclusive result from *Pathfinder*'s depth-charging, and the two battleships and their escort continued on course. During the day, the two destroyers

74

came alongside to be topped up with oil, and they were supplied with 300 pounds of bread and about 300 pounds of beef, mutton, ham and cheese.

A small boat with a red sail was sighted on the 21st. *Pathfinder* went to windward of it, broadside on, and drifted down to the boat to provide a lee. It contained 23 survivors of the SS *Cortona*, outward bound from Liverpool when she was torpedoed on the 11th. Efforts to save the ship had failed and on the 12th they took to the life-boat. The Master, Second and Third Officers were among the survivors, all brave, haggard-looking fellows after their nine-day ordeal in the Atlantic in choppy seas.

Derwent needed refuelling again the next day and the opportunity was taken to pass her more fresh bread and some money. The Paymaster Lieutenant wrote on the packet of money, 'Here's the dough – the bread follows.'

The weather improved, and although the 23rd was overcast it was a calm sea, and it was decided to air bedding. Messes brought up their hammocks, unlashed them, and using the top guard-rail like a clothes-line, spread the hammock, the mattress and then the blankets over the wire-rope and secured them with the lashing so that they could not blow over the side.

Somali, *Icarus* and *Foresight* joined the destroyer escort. At 1700 there was a boxing-match, the stokers versus the rest of the ship's company, and the result of eight clean, sporting bouts was a draw, four all. Next day there was an evolution of towing from ahead. It was well-organized, with preparatory drills, and it was gratifying that everyone took a genuine interest in it.

Early on Sunday 26th, the Force was seaward of the Outer Hebrides with Saint Kilda to port. It was marvellous weather, cold for July but fine and the visibility was amazing. Guns crews were exercised in high-angle firings. At 2230 the ships entered Scapa Flow, and *Nelson* did a quick secure to her buoy. Admiral Syfret came on board the next day.

A week of intense activity followed, the ship taking on stores and ammunition of all kinds up to her absolute capacity. The ammunition parties were working long hours, and the chains of men passing the boxes of foodstuffs from hand to hand, along the deck and down to the provision rooms, worked with a fast and steady rhythm. All too often one of the cardboard boxes of foodstuffs collapsed, scattering the contents, so that the system broke down; and valuable time was wasted while the individual tins and packets were gathered up. This was annoying and frustrating for everyone.

There were no Divisions on Sunday, 2 August. The ship left Scapa at 1600 with *Rodney* and five destroyers and headed south through the Minches. At a rendezvous the following day there were many old friends among a convoy of fourteen merchantmen: *Port Chalmers* (the Commodore's ship), *Brisbane Star*, *Melbourne Star*, *Dorset*, *Empire Hope*, *Rochester Castle*, *Clan Ferguson*, *Glenorchy*, *Wairangi*, *Waimarama* and *Deucalion*. Another two were American ships with American crews: the *Santa Elisa* and *Almeria Lykes*. And there was the *Ohio*, a fast American-built tanker with a British crew. She would write her own page in history.

Already escorting the convoy was Rear-Admiral Sir Harold Burrough in the cruiser *Nigeria*, and her sister ship *Kenya*, which for arctic waters was painted in a special camouflage scheme of pale pink. Brought south in a hurry, there was no time to paint ship before she became an outstanding target in the entirely different conditions of the Mediterranean. Fourteen destroyers were in position as the screen.

There were damage control exercises and as darkness came a night emergency procedure. Specially embarked were an RAF Radio Intelligence Officer, a photographer and an Admiralty Constructor. The Chief Bosun's Mate asked the Commander, 'Did you say, Sir, that he's a Constructor or an Instructor?' When Commander Blundell confirmed a Constructor, Chief Petty Officer Sadler laughed and said, 'Oh, he's one of those fellers who puts the scuppers at the highest part of the deck.'

Tuesday, 4 August, was spent in drilling the convoy. Many of the ships were old hands at the game. The exercises went with precision and at each new order the whole force turned majestically as one.

For the next three days the ship was made ready for action. The Principal Medical Officer lectured on first aid and the Constructor on damage control, and there were demonstrations of fire-fighting and drills of various kinds. Ventilation trunks were blanked off in many places and the hand-wheels removed, and middle-deck doors were welded up. All over the ship dumps of food and cigarettes were placed, even one in the Admiral's cabin aft. Never had *Nelson* been so prepared for battle.

On Saturday, 8 August, more ships joined, and officers and men stared in amazement to see five aircraft carriers steaming together. It was to become a common sight later in the war, but in 1942 it was something new and it served to underline the vital importance of the convoy and the gravity of the situation. Operation 'Pedestal' was about to begin. All was ready.

There could be no doubt that Malta was starving. Conditions in 1941 had been bad, but now the situation was desperate. When America had entered the war in December 1941, there had been a general feeling that things would soon begin to get better, but the Allies were suffering grievous losses of territory, men and materials in many parts of the world. At first, Britain even had to send anti-submarine vessels from her own slender resources to assist the Americans off their eastern coast. In the face of such sacrifice and defeat, men of the Allied nations could not even guess that the war was about to turn in their favour – the hinge of fate as Churchill called it – and that it would turn on three great battles: the British victory of El Alamein in the Western Desert, the defence of Stalingrad by the

Russians, and the American victory in the Pacific at the Battle of Midway.

For the El Alamein offensive we had to hold on to Malta, but convoys to the island had met with massive slaughter. Of a convoy from Alexandria in February 1942, not a single ship arrived. In March, another convoy sailed from Alexandria; though damaged, the *Breconshire* with a cargo of oil managed to struggle through and beach herself at Marsaxlokk at the south-eastern end of the island. Two others, *Pampas* and *Talabot*, reached Grand Harbour but they had unloaded less than a quarter of their cargo before they were sunk at their moorings. In June, six merchantmen sailed from Gibraltar and two reached the island; and a convoy of eleven which sailed from Alexandria was so mauled and in danger of being overwhelmed by the Italian main fleet that it was ordered back. Small quantities of supplies were run through at high speed by the 40-knot minelayers *Manxman* and *Welshman*, and some reached Malta by submarine.

It was not enough. The island was starving. The Governor and his staff concluded that unless a convoy could succour the island by not later than the end of the first week in September 1942, its surrender was inevitable. Humane considerations would never have counted with the Russians, or the Germans, or the Japanese, but no British Governor would allow the Maltese people to starve; those sturdy, friendly people who had already endured so much.

The British War Cabinet resolved that a convoy must succeed. To get the fourteen merchant ships through were forces totalling two battleships, five aircraft carriers, seven cruisers, 33 destroyers, six corvettes, four minesweepers, a Motor Launch Flotilla, and nine submarines on patrol. It was the largest concentration yet of British naval strength in support of a supply convoy.

When Sunday, 9 August, dawned, this formidable force was an awe-inspiring sight as it steamed in perfect order towards the Straits of Gibraltar. There was no slackening of the drills and exercises. An empty CO_2 cylinder became an unexploded bomb to be dealt with smartly. There were mock air attacks, and late in the afternoon, for the benefit of the ships' gunners, there was a recognition fly-past of an Albacore, Martlet, Hurricane, Fulmar, and even a Hudson flown out from Gibraltar. The fighters had a yellow front to their wings and a yellow tail fin. At 2330 the scene from the flagship was dramatic, a perfectly clear sky with the Milky Way banded across it and every star shining. Cape Spartel light was shining to starboard, and to port was Cape Trafalgar.

Refuelling was a major element in the planning, and while some ships went into Gibraltar for oil others were refuelled under way. A subsidiary part of the organization was Operation 'Berserk' to train the various groups to work together and in particular to train the aircraft carriers. *Victorious* had come from the Home Fleet and *Indomitable* from the Indian Ocean. Many of the pilots were newcomers and numbers of valuable aircraft were written off during this brief work-up. *Argus* was used to 'top up' the other carriers, and as the fleet entered the Mediterranean her job was finished and she left for Gibraltar. The air defence of the convoy now rested upon the 72 fighters aboard *Eagle*, *Indomitable* and *Victorious*. *Furious* was ferrying RAF aircraft for Malta and when she was within 550 miles of the island she was due to fly off 38 Spitfires.

Monday, 10 August was Day One of Operation 'Pedestal'. At 0800 the masters of the merchant ships opened sealed orders and read this letter from the First Lord of the Admiralty:

Before you start on this operation the First Sea Lord and I are anxious that you should know how grateful the Board of Admiralty are to you for undertaking this difficult task. Malta has for some time been in great danger. It is imperative that she should be kept supplied. These are her critical months and we cannot fail her. She has stood up to the most violent attack from the air that has ever been made; and now she needs our help in

79

continuing the battle. Her courage is worthy of yours.

We know that Admiral Syfret will do all he can to complete the operation with success, and that you will stand by him according to the splendid traditions of the Merchant Navy. We wish you all God speed and good luck.

To all ships in the convoy, Admiral Syfret made the following signal:

The garrison and people of Malta, who have been defending their island so gallantly against incessant attacks by the German and Italian air forces, are in urgent need of replenishments of food and military supplies. These we are taking to them and I know that every officer and man in the convoy and its escort will do his utmost to ensure that they reach Malta safely.

You may be sure that the enemy will do all in his power to prevent the convoy getting through and it will require every exertion on our part to see that he fails in his attempt. During the next few days all ships will be in the first and second degree of readiness for long periods. When you are on watch be especially vigilant and alert, and, for that reason, when you are off duty, get all the sleep you can. Every one of us must give of his best. Malta looks to us for help. We shall not fail them.

Throughout the day there was a stiff breeze from the east. It was uneventful except for a number of air alarms, and most of these turned out to be RAF aircraft which had failed to identify themselves.

In the early hours of Tuesday the 11th, enemy submarine activity was reported and there was some depth-charging at about 0500. Three hours later a corvette sighted two torpedoes breaking surface, and at about the same time the first snooping enemy aircraft were picked up by radar. Late in the forenoon there was another submarine attack and *Nelson*'s look-outs reported what looked like a torpedo breaking surface at a distance of three miles. The cruiser *Charybdis* made a similar report.

Shortly after midday, *Furious* altered course to fly off her aircraft from the convoy's port wing. The first flight of eight Spitfires was airborne by 1230 and the other groups followed

Above: Cleaning out. A brass tampion with
Nelson's head is being held in front of the left
gun of 'B' turret. In the muzzle of the centre gun
of 'A' turret is a pisaba brush; sometimes,
instead of the brush, a man was pulled through
the barrel. 1930. (RAF Museum)
Below: Church of Saint Christopher, HMS
Nelson. The screen was later removed and
stained-glass windows were fitted inside the
scuttles. 1932. (RAF Museum)

Above: Hoisting the picket-boat by main derrick. A man on P3 turret holds the stern-rope: it was usual to let painter and stern-rope hang down so that they could be used as steadying lines. 1932. (RAF Museum)

Below: The damaged flagship. She is holed forward port side, and down by the bows. 1941. (IWM)

Opposite, top: Air attack. As the Italian aircraft crosses *Nelson*'s bows the splash of its torpedo seen on the right. A few seconds later the torpe. struck. 1941. (IWM)

Opposite, centre: Back at Gibraltar, the Torped. Officer surveys the wreckage of *Nelson*'s 24.5-inch torpedoes. 1941. (Captain Blundell's Collection)

Above and below: Operation 'Pedestal'. Under attack. 1942. (IWM)

Top: *Nelson*'s night barrage off Salerno, seen from the aircraft carrier HMS *Illustrious*. (William Kimber)

Above: General Dwight D. Eisenhower and Admiral Sir Andrew Cunningham on board at Algiers. Vice-Admiral Sir Algernon Willis, Flag Officer Force 'H', is on the right. 1943. (IWM)

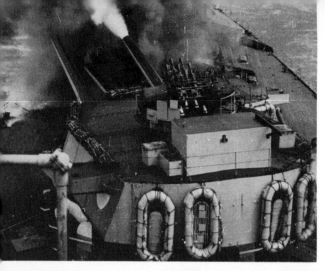

Left: 'B' Turret of the main armament. 1944. (Author's Collection)
Below: Port 6-inch Battery. 1944. (Author's Collection)
Bottom: The challenge in the Ionian Sea. As the British and American Armies make their first landings on Italian soil in southern Sicily, the battleships of Force 'H' are between them and the Italian Fleet. Left to Right: *Valiant, Nelson* (Flag), *Rodney* and *Warspite*. 1943. (IWM)

Right: Exercising in preparation for the Far East, 14-inch shells from *Anson* straddle *Nelson*'s line of advance in a throw-off shoot. The ship's bows are about to enter the ripples of the last salvo. 1945. (Author's Collection)

Below: HMS *Nelson* arrives on the East Indies Station to become Flagship, Third Battle Squadron. 1945. (IWM)

Left: At the table where two years earlier the surrender of Italy was signed, Rear-Admiral Uozumi signs for Japan the surrender of Penang. 1945. (Author's Collection)
Below: Victory Parade, Penang Men of HMS *Nelson* pass Vice-Admiral Walker at the saluting base. 1945. (Author's Collection)
Bottom: At Neptune's Court, Captain Caslon is awarded the Southern Cross and Polar Star. 1945. (Author's Collection)

at intervals. In all 37 of the 38 she carried arrived safely in Malta. In a short while *Furious* would be escorted back to Gibraltar, there to collect another 23 Spitfires which she would fly off for the island on 17 August.

At 1315 a German submarine penetrated the screen and from a range of 500 yards fired four torpedoes at *Eagle*. In *Nelson*, the first anyone knew of it was the sight of the old carrier listing rapidly to port. No noise was heard in the flagship. One moment all was serene, a blue sea and peaceful ships, the next billows of smoke from *Eagle*, funnel gas probably, and then she was going over, aircraft tumbling like small toys into the sea from her canting flight deck. All four torpedoes had smashed into her port side, she rolled gently on her side, and in about six minutes the sea closed over her and she was gone.

On *Nelson*'s upper deck a young fo'c's'leman from Birmingham named Ted Capp stood motionless, watching in horror as his brother's ship went down. Everyone thought there could be very few survivors, for she had gone so quickly, but by good fortune when he returned to Gibraltar one of the first people he saw was his brother. The Admiralty Constructor was white-faced, and all over the ship people registered shock.

The destroyers *Laforey* and *Lookout* were ordered to rescue survivors and they managed to pick up 929 from the complement of 1,160.

The Force made a number of emergency turns as other ships claimed submarine contacts, and a torpedo track was reported ahead of *Victorious*. About an hour later attention was switched to the air as radar reported the approach of enemy aircraft. Flying at a great height, the German Junkers Ju 88s, apparently on photographic reconnaissance, made no attempt to attack. The British fighters were unable to reach them, but *Rodney* and *Nelson* fired a number of rounds of 4.7-inch shell which seemed to do no more than express an opinion.

At the approach of dusk, Admiral Syfret signalled the

leading destroyers to increase their distance to 6,000 yards ahead of the convoy. *Victorious* and *Indomitable* turned into wind and flew off all available fighters.

Commander Blundell had planned to give a last pep-talk over the tannoy that evening, but it was not to be. The alarm rattlers sounded as thirty Junkers Ju 88s attacked on the port side, and then came the Heinkel torpedo bombers roaring in at mast height.

The approaching aircraft were met by a barrage of gunfire unparalleled in the experience of anyone there. Some of the German pilots, well-trained as they were, turned aside to seek lesser targets. And some came on, into the ferocious, deadly curtain of bursting shells. The ship was near-missed by two torpedoes, one forward (its bubble-track appeared to go under the hull) and one aft which seemed to miss by only a few feet. Bombs fell all over the place, and after one turn to port, a large bomb fell exactly between *Nelson* and *Rodney*.

Commander Blundell recorded his impression in words which, more than forty years later, may seen strange; they certainly represent one of the paradoxes of war:

> When it got darkish about 2115 the barrage put up by the fleet and screen was aesthetically one of the weirdest and most wonderful and beautiful sights I have ever seen. People who had been up on the SP Deck [Signal Projection Deck] and seen it all had a look on their faces as if they'd seen a vision – the sort of look a man would have on his face just after he'd looked on the Almighty. It was the purple sea and the black sky and the red in the west, and the panels of rubies of the tracer necklaces and the lurid bursts in the sky and the dark little ships putting up this miracle display.

People in other ships close by were equally affected as they watched *Nelson* put up her huge umbrella to cover the fleet. To them, *Nelson* seemed one mass of stabbing flashes from end to end with streams of sparks racing into the sky, with even the 16-inch main armament adding to the barrage.

Strangely, even above the thunder of the armament the

wail of the sirens calling for emergency turns could still be heard, and the darkening shapes of the warships and their charges turned majestically in perfect order as surely as if they were practising in calmer waters.

The action lasted about two hours. At the end of that time darkness was complete and the enemy made no further air attack until daylight came.

Wednesday, 12 August, was a critical day for the operation. The ship was closed up all day at first degree of AA readiness, including the 16-inch loaded with barrage shell set to burst at 3,000 feet. There was action messing and the gunners ate at the guns during lulls in the battle.

Both battleships fired main armament barrages against enemy planes. One moment the torpedo bombers were racing in a few feet above the surface, the next there was a huge splash just in front of them as the shells exploded, each shell weighing 2,461 pounds. When the smoke cleared and spray subsided, there were some planes turning away. They were not seen again.

The carrier aircraft were superb, breaking up most of the enemy formations as they approached the convoy. Those that got through faced a severe dusting from the destroyer screen, and if they penetrated the heart of the convoy they encountered the furious barrages of the heavy ships.

Nelson's close-range guns shot down three in rapid succession. The enemy managed to drop many bombs close to her and there were three very near misses in one attack, but they failed to score a hit. *Deucalion* was badly damaged by a near miss and had to drop astern. She was told to try to creep along inshore at her best speed, but was later detected and sent to the bottom by torpedo.

Just after 1830 a particularly fierce attack developed. First came a formation of thirteen torpedo planes on the starboard bow, and once again the effectiveness of accurate barrage firing was demonstrated and the formation was broken up. Then about twelve Junkers Ju 87s came down on *Indomitable*, catching her at the wrong angle. The Stuka dive-bombers hurtled down out of the sun, and for what seemed several minutes nothing could be seen but bursting bombs and columns of water where the carrier had been. Eventually the maelstrom subsided and there was the *Indomitable* blazing fore and aft with enormous columns of smoke pouring out of her.

Her fighting potential was gone. Her casualties were terrible. The off-duty pilots and observers were in the wardroom and not one survived.

The Admiral feared that the enemy would make every effort to finish the carrier off and immediately ordered *Nelson* and *Rodney* to shield her from further attack. It was, in any case, nearing the time when the big ships would have to leave the convoy to complete their run through with only the close escort under Rear-Admiral Burrough for protection.

For the time being the battleships and carriers marked time, together with the cruisers *Charybdis*, *Scylla* and *Phoebe*, and destroyers. Up to this moment no merchant ship had been sunk; Admiral Syfret wished them 'God Speed' and the convoy drew away to the east.

Aboard *Indomitable* herculean efforts were being made with essential repairs to save her from further harm. The fires were brought under control, and through the strenuous work of the engine-room she was able to report by 2030 that she could steam at 28 knots.

Grave though her damage was, and coupled with the loss of the *Eagle* this meant that only *Victorious* could now operate aircraft, everyone felt some surprise and quiet satisfaction that the merchantmen had suffered no loss in the face of such massive attacks from above and below the sea. From now on it would be a very different story.

Lying in wait to the east were more patrol lines of submarines, and E-boats (the enemy's motor torpedo-boats); and the German and Italian air forces were determined upon the annihilation of the convoy.

At 1955, the Italian submarine *Axum* (Tenente di

Vascello Renato Ferrini) fired four torpedoes with devastating effect. Two hit the cruiser *Cairo*, one hit Rear-Admiral Burrough's flagship *Nigeria*, and the fourth struck the only tanker in the convoy, the *Ohio*. Burrough transferred his flag to the destroyer *Ashanti*. From the fleet flagship, Admiral Syfret at once detached the cruiser *Charybdis* and destroyers *Eskimo* and *Somali* from his own force and they went off at high speed to reinforce the convoy escort.

Only about half an hour later the last air attack of the day was made. The *Empire Hope* was left ablaze and sinking, *Brisbane Star* was hit, the ammunition ship *Clan Ferguson* exploded, and the *Rochester Castle* was left leaking from near misses.

The next submarine in their path was the Italian *Alagi* (Tenente di Vascello Sergio Puccini) and at about 2100 she fired four torpedoes. One struck the bows of the cruiser *Kenya* causing severe damage.

As Day Three of the operation came to an end, the convoy was rounding Cape Bon. Just round the corner were the E-boats, and the first casualty of Day Four, Thursday, 13 August, was the cruiser *Manchester*. At 0107 two Italian E-boats attacked her with torpedoes and she suffered mortal damage. Two hours later, another attack by the E-boats developed, *Wairangi* was torpedoed, and then the American *Santa Elisa* which burst into flames from end to end.

The slaughter went on. During the forenoon, Admiral Syfret decided to send some of his lame ducks back to Gibraltar. *Rodney* had been experiencing boiler trouble, and with her he sent *Indomitable* and the destroyer *Ithuriel* which had damaged her bows when she rammed and sank the Italian submarine *Cobalto*. Five destroyers were detailed to escort them.

Nelson patrolled with *Victorious* off the African coast, waiting to assist the damaged *Kenya*. Signals came in recording one tragic loss after another. Of Rear-Admiral Burrough's four cruisers, two were sunk and two damaged. After the convoy's initial success, the sinking of the merchantmen was heart-breaking. Only five of the fourteen succeeded in reaching Malta: *Port Chalmers*, *Ohio*, *Brisbane Star*, *Melbourne Star* and *Rochester Castle*. *Ohio* was torpedoed, set on fire, an enemy plane crashed on her decks, she was hit by a bomb, and another plane struck her. But she crawled into Grand Harbour, almost awash, supported by a ship on either side, and with most of her precious cargo of fuel oil intact. She never sailed again. After the war her wreck was taken to sea for burial close to the island for whose life she gave her all. Her master, Captain Mason, richly merited the award of the George Cross.

The people of Malta called it the Santa Marija Convoy, coinciding with nine days of prayer ending on the Feast of the Assumption, 15 August, the day on which the *Ohio* struggled in. One cannot hope to recapture its full meaning and emotional content for the Maltese. As the first ships entered Grand Harbour there were bands playing and thousands of cheering, waving people. They were every-where, in the streets and along the bastions, in the Barracca Gardens, at windows and along the foreshore.

One eye-witness described a group whose cheering faded into silence as the people noticed the twisted steel and scarred decks of the few surviving ships. Out of the depths of their own suffering from countless air raids, they realised what a terrible gauntlet the convoy had run.

On Friday, 14 August, Admiral Syfret received a signal at about 1500 from Rear-Admiral Commanding 10th Cruiser Squadron (Burrough) and the two forces met during the evening. Gibraltar was in sight at about 1800 the following day and *Nelson* berthed bows south at the south mole an hour later. It was remarked that Captain Jacomb put her alongside like a picket-boat. 'E's a boy, that Captain, a'nt 'e!', was one comment.

For the most part there was a feeling of depression about the operation and the terrible losses. 'The Navy thrives on impossibilities,' said the BBC commentator. 'Yes, but for how long?,' men questioned. Not until the autumn came, when the Western Desert was finally cleared of the enemy, and British and American forces landed in North Africa, did the men of *Nelson* appreciate what had been achieved in fighting those few supply ships through to Malta.

All the commanding officers in the fleet came on board for a conference on Sunday, 16 August. Two days later a large number of survivors from other ships joined.

On Thursday the 20th, three Italian officers and 36 Italian rating prisoners of war came on board. The officers were put in a cabin in the Midshipmen's Chest Flat, the Chief and Petty Officers in the Cell Flat, and the ratings in the Salvage Office and the Damage Control Workshop. The guards put in charge of them were all survivors from *Eagle* and *Manchester*. At 2100 the ship prepared for sea and singled-up wires, at 2130 a number of officer passengers, including *Eagle* survivors, arrived and the ship sailed at 0230 on the 21st in company with the damaged *Kenya* and the aircraft carriers *Argus* and *Furious*.

The journey home was uneventful, except that speed had to be reduced to fifteen knots because *Kenya*'s damaged bow opened up and her capstan machinery room was flooded. Mist and fog came down, concealing the body of ships, and fog buoys were streamed.

They arrived off Greenock at 1225 on Tuesday, 25 August, and anchored. The arrangements made to receive them were most efficient, a drifter and a large ferry took the survivors away quickly and easily, and the Army came to collect the prisoners of war at 1800. But there was no mail – someone had bungled that very important item.

During the next fortnight, the ship proceeded to Scapa and then to Rosyth, where she arrived, passing *Rodney*, *Victorious* and *Formidable*, on Saturday, 19 September. The first leave party was away on the 21st and next day she was docked for a short refit.

By 16 October she was back at Scapa and exercises began. On the 24th she did a 16-inch throw-off shoot, 4.7-inch anti E-boat firings, 6-inch and 16-inch night bombardments of

Stack Skerry with aircraft spotting and dropping flares over the target, then a night target shoot using starshell and salvos of 16-inch and 6-inch. The new flashless starshell ammunition was very effective and the bridge personnel could not see the gun go off. Finally, there were night anti E-boat firings and everyone was pleased with the results of this large programme.

The morning of the 26th began with howling wind and rain squalls. At 0740 ships were coming from all directions. The store-ship *Robert Dundas* was first and did a wonderful alongside, just missing the after ladder. Next came an ammunition ship, the *Syrian Prince*, which carried away two stanchions; then the water-boat, and two other ammunition ships. Eventually, the whole unruly brood quietened down.

No 9 Commando arrived from Dorchester two days later, 400 fine, well-disciplined men, and their officers were most helpful. At 1715 they were fallen in on the upper deck with all their gear and weapons, and six folding boats. 'You could put the 'ole lot in a registered envelope,' said the Chief Bosun's Mate. All six boats stowed absolutely flat one on top of the other, and they were put on top of 'X' turret as a parcel measuring 20 feet by 6 feet by 3 feet.

There was no shore leave the following day and *Nelson* sailed on Friday, 30 October, at 1645, in company with *Duke of York* and *Renown*, and the cruiser *Argonaut*. Destroyers took up their positions and the Force pitched and rolled heavily through the Pentlands. Behind them *King George V*, *Anson* and *Howe* also came out to do a shoot at Skerry Vore.

The Commando Orders posted the following day caused much amusement by the inclusion of this paragraph:

'All ranks are advised that should a man fall overboard while *Nelson* is at sea, the ship cannot, and will not, attempt to stop and pick him up. Every precaution should therefore be taken by personnel not to fall overboard.'

During the day the aircraft carriers *Illustrious* and *Formidable* joined, details were announced of Operation

'Torch' to land British and American forces in North Africa. In the operation orders, *Nelson* was referred to as 'spare battleship' and this explained why Vice-Admiral Syfret was flying his flag in the fast battleship *Duke of York*. The flagship and *Renown* put into Gibraltar Bay to re-fuel on 5 November, while *Nelson* stayed at sea with the two carriers, and then it was *Nelson*'s turn early the next morning.

She passed the breakwater at 0515 in such intense darkness that it was quite impossible to see the bow or stern from the bridge. The Petty Officers had to use hand-torches to muster the men. Because the tugs were late the ship started to turn on her own, and there was a wrenching of wires and crashing of timber as the ship's stem touched a group of small craft which were lying between the depot ship *Maidstone* and two large tankers. Nevertheless, she berthed without difficulty and breakfast was piped at 0700.

The Commandos started to go ashore, there were numbers of air raid alarms, and in the afternoon an enormous convoy came through the Straits. The airfield at Gibraltar was crammed with aircraft wing tip to wing tip with just a small space left as a runway. News of the Alamein battle was good.

There was a red air warning at 0500 on Sunday, 8 November, and some shore guns opened fire, but that was all. The Captain broadcast a message from Admiral Sir Andrew Cunningham, and at 0800 Sir Andrew hoisted his flag in *Nelson* as Commander-in-Chief, Mediterranean, in charge of all naval forces for the operation.

The BBC gave news of the landings at Algiers, Oran and Casablanca in French territory, and announced that the American General Eisenhower was in command of all the Allied forces. Although there were some mishaps, in general the operation was going very well, a triumph of organization involving 500 merchant ships and 350 warships. The outstanding factor was the lightness of merchant ship casualties.

There was no hint of intervention by either the French fleet at Toulon or the Italians at Taranto. The Germans, however, marched into the unoccupied zone of France, and poured more troops and planes into Tunisia to counter the Allied stroke. Most would be taken prisoner.

In places the French resisted the landings, but after three days Admiral Darlan ordered the French forces to lay down their arms.

On Sunday, 15 November, *Nelson* resumed duty as Flagship, Force 'H', when Vice-Admiral Syfret and his staff came on board, and she sailed from Gibraltar the following day with *Rodney* and the aircraft carriers *Formidable* and *Furious*. On the 18th she entered Mers-el-Kebir. Some damage from Allied bombardment was evident, but the general impression of the place was that it spoke of North Africa: the scrub, the blue sky and deep blue sea, and a Beau Geste-type fort at the western end – it was all yellows and blues.

Extreme precautions had to be taken by all the ships in harbour against human torpedoes and explosive charges on the bottom.

By the 22nd the ship was back at Gibraltar, and then again at Mers-el-Kebir on the 25th. Next day she sailed to cover a cruiser force which was hoping to intercept Italian convoys to Bizerta and Tunis, and then she went north on the 27th to be nearer the French at Toulon, as German troops were entering the town and it was thought possible that some of the French ships might try to make a run for it.

Next day, as she patrolled south of the Balearics, radar picked up a German Junkers Ju 88 bomber. He seemed to be a bit lost because of cloud and obviously had not spotted the fleet. *Nelson*'s guns tracked him until he suddenly appeared in a break in the clouds. The pom-poms opened a furious and deadly fire, and the German aircraft burst into flames and plummeted into the sea with a great splash.

The ship was back in Mers-el-Kebir on 30 November. There was so much to do: Commanding Officers of ships arriving all the time to see the Admiral or Chief of Staff, boards of enquiry, examination boards, small ships alongside to be fed, buoys to be laid, arrangements to be made for the disposal of gash, Americans and French to be received on board. One day a party of American nurses arrived, nice, cheerful girls who said they had not tasted fresh white bread since they had left the States, and did full justice to their meal on board.

As the ship left harbour on 4 December, the Army hospital ship *Newfoundland* was coming in and a collision very nearly occurred. *Nelson* gave two short blasts to show she was edging over to port, but the other gave one short blast and altered course right across the battleship's bows. Everyone was ordered off the fo'c's'le and one of the officers commented, 'We'll never stop her now.' The Captain had already gone full astern, however. He never raised his voice at all, but quietly conned her out of a possible disaster. The two ships were dangerously close, but all the wounded soldiers and the nurses were leaning over the rails and smiling as if everything were quite normal. The comment of Chief Petty Officer Sadler, the Chief Bosun's Mate, was, 'I reckon we were looking Rosyth Dockyard right in the face.'

There was a human torpedo attack on 8 December while the ship was at Gibraltar, and at 0430 rockets went up, searchlights scanned the harbour and depth-charges were dropped. It seemed that only one torpedo penetrated the harbour, and that the two-man crew were knocked off their perch by the depth-charging, came to the surface and were captured. Blindfolded, they were put in the bottom of *Furious* to encourage them to talk.

It was obvious that the job of Flagship, Force 'H' was now quite different from the role in 1941. The perilous Malta convoys were in the past and she had become a mother hen looking after the massive naval forces in the area. When she next arrived at Mers-el-Kebir on 11 December, she brought a large number of berthing wires and catamaran lanyards, 6,000 blocks of TNT for the Naval Officer in Charge, mail for the *Vindictive*, an oerlikon gun for the *Clan McIver*, as well as supplying food and oil to a number of ships, and taking aboard sixty survivors from the *Porcupine*.

There had also been a marked change in her ship's company. A year ago there had been very few 'hostilities only' ratings, but now there were increasing numbers of wartime volunteers and conscripts in all Departments. On one occasion a destroyer was having difficulty in mooring and the Commander hailed her and asked whether she would find it easier to lie alongside *Nelson*. The destroyer Captain was happy to accept and as he brought his ship in, the Commander turned to a rating in seaman's rig nearby and said, 'Pull in the grass through the fairlead and put the bight on the bollard.' The man did not move. As seconds counted, the Commander took the rope himself and, afterwards, the rating said in an apologetic, cultured voice, 'I'm terribly sorry, Sir, I hadn't the faintest idea what you meant.' It turned out that the man was a professor of mathematics from Cambridge entered specially as a 'Y' rating (not to be confused with the 'Y' Entry Scheme for officer selection) for breaking enemy codes.

The British Naval Liaison Officer ashore had at his disposal a very unreliable boat named the *Sacré Coeur de Jean*. 'It's just too sacred to go!,' he explained.

A number of invitations were received from the US General Fredenhall. At dinner, Admiral Syfret's Secretary was sitting next to another American General who suddenly asked, 'Say, who is that French Admiral sitting opposite?' The Secretary answered, 'Why, that is your own Admiral in command, Admiral Bennett,' to which the American General replied, 'Say, am I embarrassed.'

Later on the same day, three big troopships came in with more Allied troops. A fourth, the *Strathallan*, had been torpedoed and the survivors were picked up by destroyers. *Verity* came in crammed with the unbelievable number of 1,200; everyone thought she was going to roll over, and then *Panther* came in with 1,700.

Mers-el-Kebir was a restless place and an uneasy anchorage. When there was a shift of wind of Force 4 or more, a stream (or stern) anchor simply would not hold. At a Commanding Officers' conference on 23 December, the Captain commented what an awful harbour it was. Five minutes later the cable of the stream anchor parted, then a French oiler struck the ship's port quarter. Luckily, the stream anchor had been buoyed. In pouring rain, the cutter was rigged as a diving boat, and the diver, Petty Officer Thornton, reported that the anchor was completely buried in thirteen fathoms. He was told to try to follow the shank and to shackle a 4-inch berthing wire on to the ring of the anchor. This he eventually managed to do.

A tug towed *Nelson* round until the stern was over the anchor, the end of the 4-inch wire was passed up on to the quarterdeck, brought to the after capstan, and the anchor weighed. It was a lesson always to have a watch buoy with a good hemp line. The same day, as if to confirm the Captain's verdict, a French gash boat savaged one of the quarter booms.

Nelson proceeded to sea at 1000 the following day and set course for Algiers where Flag Officer, Force 'H', was to meet Admiral Cunningham. Preparations for Christmas Day were in full swing, the next day's daily orders were being produced with a decoration of holly and other Christmas designs in coloured inks, and Sub-Lieutenant Whalley had produced a 'Nelson's Xmas Rag'.

In the early hours of 25 December a signalman woke Commander Blundell with the message that the ship was not to go to Algiers but was to remain at sea. The French Admiral Darlan had been assassinated. The Commander's greatest disappointment was that the ship's company would not now be able to have scuttles and deadlights open on the mess-decks, nor would the Captain be able to do the traditional Christmas rounds.

Instead of Dawn Action Stations, the ship stood to the watch and at 0800 both watches cleaned mess-decks, rigged church on the upper deck, after which the men started to decorate the mess-decks and quite a fever of competition started. Church was at 0930, and at 1045 the Commander made a very informal tour of the messes which were marvellously decorated with paper balls and streamers, and flags everywhere; and there were oranges, dates and raisins to supplement the Christmas dinner. Various messes offered invitations, and at 1130 a party of Chief and Petty Officers was entertained in the wardroom. The wardroom lunch was a buffet affair so that the wardroom attendants could enjoy their Christmas dinner without interruption.

The ship berthed at Gibraltar at dusk on Saturday, 26 December. Instead of Divisions next day, everyone was involved in storing ship. On Thursday, 31 December, it snowed, something almost unheard of at Gibraltar. Thoughts turned to a better 1943, toasts were drunk, and at midnight Midshipman Mackilligan rang sixteen bells.

4

Assault on Europe

On New Year's Day, 1943, *Nelson*'s wartime mileage totalled 102,614. From Gibraltar, the snow on top of the African hills could be clearly seen, and on the Rock itself all the open spaces were thickly carpeted with narcissi.

She sailed next morning at 0300 and arrived about midday at Algiers, which looked very fine from the sea with a vast array of white hotel fronts spread up the slope of the town. As the ship was entering harbour there was a sudden air alarm and fire was opened on a German Junkers Ju 88, but a curt signal from the aircraft carrier *Formidable* said it was an RAF Mosquito, which caused some consternation.

There was a big swell in the anchorage and Sub-Lieutenant S. Richards, RNVR, had an interested audience as he worked main derrick to get the boats out. The problem was that, with the ship rolling, the huge derrick might become uncontrollable and go smashing from side to side (as it did quite suddenly during a middle watch between Aden and Colombo in 1945, and the emergency party had to be mustered to tame the beast). The derrick was a spar about as long as a 16-inch gun barrel and as bulky as the muzzle end. Jointed to the mainmast by a swivel called a gooseneck, the other end was controlled vertically by a topping lift; also at the derrick head hung the purchase to raise or lower the load. The topping lift and purchase were both worked by power, but movement of the derrick from side to side by four guys (port fore, port after, starboard fore, starboard after) was done entirely by groups of ratings manning the hauling parts of the tackles, run through leading blocks. The ship's company humorously considered the whole archaic

95

arrangement to be a deliberate attempt to keep a bit of Nelson's Navy alive in the 20th century.

For the officer-in-charge, it was not sufficient simply to order, 'Lower topping lift, handsomely.' He had to add, 'Tend your guys, derrick lowering,' and the men on the guys had to act smartly to take up the slack, otherwise the derrick might start to swing and take charge. Having lifted a boat on its slings, it had to be taken sideways over the 6-inch gun turrets (and, after the 1944 refit, over the 'G' battery of oerlikons) before being lowered into the water. For this, the order might be, 'Haul away, port fore guy, check away starboard after,' and once the massive spar and a 10-ton boat were swinging round this would be continued with, 'Haul away, port after guy, check away starboard.' All the time, the four guys had to have no slack. Sub-Lieutenant Richards became one of the most skilful officers at handling the 'main stick', and by the war's end one of the most popular and most respected.

The ship was back at Gibraltar on 5 January and at Mers-el-Kebir on the 13th. Each harbour demanded certain chores. At Mers-el-Kebir, *Nelson* had to provide a party to man a shore searchlight, another for mine-watching, yet another to patrol the shore at night. The Americans took over the searchlights on the 19th and celebrated by firing white rockets which signalled a human torpedo alert. The 'intruder' was a wooden crate floating in the harbour entrance. The next day there was an air raid and bombs were dropped between Oran and Mers-el-Kebir. An impressive amount of tracer was pumped into the sky by *Formidable*'s pom-poms and by American Bofors on shore; and it was strange how everyone in *Nelson* seemed happier when they heard the crack of their own 4.7s adding to the din.

During the middle watch on Saturday, 23 January, Admiral Syfret began to suffer severe abdominal pains. By 0500 they were intense but he did not wish to wake his steward and it was 0800 before a doctor was called. A second opinion from *Formidable*'s Senior Medical Officer confirmed that it was appendicitis and after a hurried consultation it was decided to operate on board. He was taken from his cabin, along the main deck passage port side, through the sick bay flat to the operating room. When it was all successfully over, many people agreed that the procession forward looked like a funeral cortege and was very funny. The outriders were the Master-at-Arms and the Sick Berth Chief Petty Officer, then came Royal Marine orderlies carrying the bier, the principal mourners were the Chief of Staff, Admiral's Secretary, Flag Lieutenant and a collection of doctors, and then came a ragged tail of the household brigade.

The operation was carried out by Surgeon Lieutenant Paul Houghton MB, FRCS, RNVR, an operation made more difficult because the organ had burst and he was faced with peritonitis. Some time after the Admiral had been returned to his cabin, the doctor went with another officer to see him. He lay perfectly still. Just inside the door was the Admiral's telescope. Lifting it from its hooks and peering through it the wrong way, Lieutenant Houghton exclaimed, 'Oh, Joe, it looks like the death of Nelson to me!' From beneath the sheets came a faint, thin voice, 'Not yet, my boy, not yet.'

Two days later the hospital ship *Oxfordshire* came alongside, bow to stern. Admiral Syfret was brought up on a stretcher which was placed on a platform with slings, and when all was ready, he was hoisted gently by the ship's crane up to the *Oxfordshire*'s boat deck. It had to go to an immense height to clear her davits, and everyone felt a sense of relief when the Admiral was safely aboard the hospital ship.

On Tuesday, 26 January, the ship went to two hours' notice for sea as Allied reconnaissance had lost track of the Italian battleship *Littorio*, last seen at La Spezia. All shore leave was stopped. To replace Admiral Syfret temporarily, Rear-Admiral Burrough came on board, two hours' notice was cancelled, and on the 29th the new Admiral inspected the ship's company. Pulling races were at this time producing a lot of friendly rivalry between divisions and on 2 February there was an exciting final of the cutter races in which the fo'c's'lemen beat the officers.

Nelson left Mers-el-Kebir at 1130 on Sunday, 7 February, and arrived at Gibraltar the following day. For the next four days she had a hectic programme of storing ship, and in the middle of it all an Army contingent of four officers and 60 men, 75 tons of stores and four small trucks arrived for transport to North Africa. The clutter on the upper deck was extreme, with masses of barbed wire, milk, flour and bacon, timber, explosives, radio equipment and potatoes, plus the vehicles. At midday on Friday 12th, it looked as if she would never be ready for sea, but by 1730 everything had been squared off and secured. She left harbour at 1830.

The Army disembarked at Mers-el-Kebir the following day. In that difficult anchorage there were daily anxieties, the stream anchor wire parted again and for a second time the anchor was recovered.

At 1030 on Wednesday, 17 February, Captain The Honourable Guy Russell, CBE joined, a tall, impressive-looking man. He had come to succeed Captain Jacomb who took his departure at 1400. The officers had intended to pull him away in the cutter, but the weather was too bad. As the *Monarch*, in which he was taking passage, left harbour, *Nelson* signalled, 'We all wish you God speed, a safe journey and best wishes for the future.' He responded, 'Thank you. Good fortune to you always.'

Probably the worst experience of conditions at Mers-el-Kebir came the following day. The wind was from the north, the weather worsening, and at 1700 the destroyer *Ashanti* rode up and nearly touched. She changed her billet. *Eskimo* and *Tartar* came dangerously close on the starboard side, and the heel of the starboard lower boom nearly punched a hole in *Eskimo*'s side. Minutes later, the liner *Empress of Australia* parted one of her wires, and *Nelson* fell in the duty part of the watch to work main derrick and start getting the boats in.

At 1730 a Liberty ship (a standard wartime design of merchant ship for prefabricated mass production) broke adrift from the mole and anchored off. The *Empress of Australia* went on parting wires and broke completely adrift at 1815. *Ashanti* had to get out of the way in a hurry and slipped both her anchors, to be recovered later. The three *Tribal* destroyers then put to sea to avoid further danger in the harbour. The *Empress of Australia* put two anchors down and managed to pull up short of *Nelson*, which had already veered nearly a shackle of cable on both anchors and as a further precaution had closed watertight doors and put fenders over the bows. At about 1900 another Liberty ship parted her bow wires, and then her stern wires, drifted away from her berth, got her anchors down, but dragged down *Nelson*'s starboard side some fifty yards off, eventually holding.

The situation at 2000 was pretty chaotic with the harbour full of wreckage, wood, crates and oil drums, much of which had been washed off the breakwater. *Empress of Australia* was almost dead ahead, yawing about 60° and liable to drag down on to *Nelson* at any moment. *Nelson* had all boats in and booms and ladders hoisted, all men returned from shore, officer of the watch on the bridge, six boilers connected and the cable party on the fo'c's'le; but there was half a turn in the cables, and the starboard anchor was to port and the port anchor to starboard. In any case she was completely hemmed in by other ships all trying to sort out their own problems.

Everyone spent an anxious night. At 0430 on the 19th the weather started to moderate, one by one the ships disentangled themselves and went out of harbour, and finally all was clear.

Gibraltar was a welcome change and on Tuesday, 2 March, Vice-Admiral Sir Algernon Willis arrived as the new Flag Officer, Force 'H', and Rear-Admiral Burrough departed. There was little change in the flagship's duties and she continued to patrol the western Mediterranean ready to counter any move by Italian heavy units, went back and forth between Gibraltar and North Africa, and worked in a number of exercises and practice shoots.

On 16 March, an SOS from the tug *Restive* was followed by a request for a boarding-party for a torpedoed merchant-man, the *Hadley*, which had been abandoned and which she had in tow. *Nelson* quickly sent two officers and eight men. Just a week later, a human torpedo attack on Mers-el-Kebir put the whole fleet on operation alert. The excitement went on all night with search-lights, rockets, Very lights, bursts of pom-pom and rifle fire, and tons of explosives were detonated under water. The Chief Engineer was heard to exclaim, 'Oh, my poor rivets!'

Force 'H' was at Algiers on Tuesday, 6 April, and the Admiral went to see the Commander-in-Chief, Admiral Cunningham. Later the Captain also went ashore to see Lord Gort, Governor of Malta, who had come for a brief visit. Next day, at Mers-el-Kebir, the Turkish General Saleh Omartak was received on board and *Formidable*'s aircraft put on a wonderful show for him.

Wednesday, 14 April, was the Captain's birthday and the ship's company sent him a card and a large bun suitably decorated by the baker. The ship put to sea at 0740 with *Rodney* for gunnery exercises, and then set course for Gibraltar. By the dog watches heavy seas were coming on board, great twenty to thirty feet high waves coming up from aft and very steep-fronted. She arrived at 0900 the next morning in tremendous wind squalls and heavy rain. The Captain handled her splendidly, did a perfect turn in spite of the wind, and ran alongside and secured in just 35 minutes from entering harbour.

A large party of photographers came on board at Algiers on 4 May, and at 1240 General Eisenhower and Admiral Cunningham arrived. Major Carless, Royal Marines, was in charge of a vast Guard and the timing was perfect. The buglers on top of the conning tower sounded the 'Alert' as the barge pointed for the gangway, the Guard sloped arms and the first 'Pipe the Side' ended just as the boat arrived alongside. The second 'Pipe the Side' ended, and the Guard presented arms, as the personages came into view at the head of the gangway, and as they stepped on to the brass name-plate at the ship's side the musical salute was played. Admiral Willis greeted his visitors, the Royal Marine Guard ordered arms and was reported to General Eisenhower for inspection. 'Guess I've never seen sailors in high collars before,' he quipped. The inspection over, the 'Carry On' was sounded and the visitors went below for lunch. Afterwards, General Eisenhower was taken forward and looked over 'B' turret, and after chatting to a number of people, and a lot of photographs had been taken, he went ashore.

Next day, Admiral Cunningham came again, and timing was again perfect and *Rule Britannia* was played as he stepped on to the plate. After inspecting the Guard there was a march past, and after a speech to the ship's company he left at 1005 for *Rodney*. During the afternoon *Rodney* was seen loading hundreds of bags of mail, and everyone assumed correctly that she was going home. Once again her old infirmity of steering trouble was making itself felt, she was leaking in the tiller flat, and was off without even stopping at Gibraltar.

Nelson left harbour at 1630, and it was a relief to be at sea again. She arrived at Gibraltar at 0100 on 7 May, but had to turn in circles as the gate in the boom was closed. The gate lights finally came on, the ship headed for the entrance, straightened up and was going hell for leather when a ship was seen ahead. The Captain went full astern, searchlight on, and there was *Acute* and all her sweepers anchored in a bunch round the north entrance. This waiting about did not please the flagship at all and she developed one of her cantankerous turns, tried to savage the frigate *Fleetwood*, then a merchant ship at the detached mole, and in all nearly hit three ships. But at last she simmered down in her usual berth. Before the night was out there was more excitement.

101

The enemy had penetrated the harbour and there were underwater explosions as limpet-charges went off under two ships.

By the middle of May the last of the German and Italian forces in the Cape Bon area had surrendered, and the enemy had been expelled from the whole of Africa.

And now it was *Nelson*'s turn to go home. On Monday, 24 May, a group of professional entertainers, including Leslie Henson, Beatrice Lillie, Vivien Leigh, and a number of others, came on board at Gibraltar and delighted the ship's company. *Howe* came in next day, everyone deduced that she was going to replace *Nelson*, and great numbers went ashore to buy bananas and oranges to take home.

Admiral Willis and his staff departed, and passengers came on board. Admiral James was put in the Admiral's cabin. As a very young child in Victorian England he had become famous as the subject of a painting called 'Bubbles' which was used widely to advertise Pears' Soap. Inevitably, he had been called 'Bubbles' James throughout his Service career. Brought back from retirement at the start of the war, he was serving as the Navy's Chief Press Liaison Officer. There were twelve other officers and 55 rating passengers, and at 2245 Colonel Peter de Havilland and Major Foster arrived with some senior German prisoners. They were Major-General Schnerrenberger, Commandant of Tunisia; Major-General Von Liebenstein, 164th Division; Major-General Von Broich of the Broich Division; Lieutenant-General Von Sponeck, 90th Light Division; and three aides-de-camp: Victor Hoffman, Karl Bock and Carl Carius.

The ship sailed at 0015 on the 26th. The Army officers looking after the prisoners used the Chief of Staff's day cabin for sleeping and the Germans the stewards' accommodation in the after lower-deck cabin flat where they were locked in at night. They exercised on deck from 1000 to 1100 and from 1400 to 1500, and for a quarter of an hour before supper. They fed in the Admiral's dining cabin, at a table brought up from the recreation space.

During the day one of the doctors solemnly announced that on 26 May 1940, Major-General Von Liebenstein had taken Calais, and that on 26 May 1943, he had taken Calomel (a purgative). The opinion was formed that the four Generals did not like Hitler, but that their aides were full-blown Nazis.

The voyage home was a flurry of preparation for docking. There were defect lists, leave tickets and ration cards to be made out, payment to be made and Gibraltar money exchanged for sterling. No one was very happy at the news that there would be only three days' leave for each watch.

At 1000 on Sunday, 30 May, the ship arrived at Plymouth and secured to a buoy just inside the breakwater. The prisoners were brought up on deck and were last seen escorted by two Lieutenant-Commanders and eight Gunner's Mates who took them off in a boat splendidly manned by Wrens. A paddle-tug and a drifter quickly took the first leave party ashore.

Nelson slipped at 1630 and went up harbour. It was a simply glorious, sunny day, the Hoe was crowded, and people were bathing everywhere. *Rodney* and a number of destroyers were in. Efficiently, the pilot turned her into the non-tidal basin lock, and from there she was warped right into No 10 dock in about one hour.

There was a tremendous amount of work to be done in the seven days allowed. She was to have a new admiral's barge and an extra motor-cutter, 25 more 20mm Oerlikons, improvements to the 16-inch and HA directors, the crane refitted, the cypher office relocated, and the ship's bottom scraped and painted.

The second leave party mustered at 2330 on 2 June and caught a train at Keyham Station at 0100. Ashore in Plymouth the crew were appalled at the destruction of the city, especially the obliteration of George Street and the Civic Centre. No vestige remained of many old landmarks.

The outstanding impression of leave parties travelling by rail was always the lush greenness of the English country-

103

side. Of Britain in general it was of the extraordinary way everything had been harnessed to the war effort; so many responsibilities now rested upon women and elderly men.

On Monday, 7 June, *Nelson* slipped at 0930 and was soon heading north for Scapa. The dockyard had done a fine job and the radar people had practically lived on board. She entered the Flow on the 9th and Admiral Willis returned on board.

A week of the most intensive exercises in company with *Rodney*, *Valiant* and *Warspite* began. Officers and men found it incredible that the main armament held the target with salvo after salvo, with the director sighting-ports closed. The new radar was achieving amazingly impressive results.

The climax to all this training as a single battle-squadron came on Wednesday, 16 June, when destroyers towed three battle-practice targets at high speed at ranges between 18,000–20,000 yards. To facilitate analysis of the fall of shot, red aniline dye was added to *Rodney*'s practice shells, blue for *Valiant* and yellow for *Warspite*. With no additive for *Nelson*, her shell bursts were white.

The battle-line completely destroyed the targets in just fifteen minutes. A night shoot followed. With morale high, everyone felt that if the Italians should come out now their ships would stand no chance at all.

At 1330 on 17 June, the fleet sailed from Scapa, the four battleships, the aircraft carrier *Indomitable* and thirteen destroyers. There were two days of mist and fog, and late on the 19th a four-engined Liberator crashed in the sea nearby and one of the destroyers picked up six survivors of its crew of eight. As the fog lifted the weather worsened until the ships were pitching and rolling in enormous seas. The starboard lower boom broke away from its new crutches, a flotanet lashed to the boat-deck guard-rails was whipped straight overboard, three Oerlikon lockers broke adrift and one went over the side, seven Oerlikon gun-shields folded together, the 4½-inch wire on its reel before 'S1' turret was uprooted, and the steel ladder to the 4.7-inch gun-deck was buckled. The weather moderated in the evening of the 21st and the fleet was able to do some exercises. It had been a fine sight to see the Force moving and plunging in the storm.

On Wednesday, 23 June, the ships arrived at Gibraltar. After the very short period of leave and the intense preparations, the ship's company expected her to be in for a day or so and then off for a big battle.

A week later everyone had a cry-wolf feeling. At 1330 on the 30th there was a sudden explosion followed by columns of smoke and flame, apparently from the coaling wharf. The stern of the patrol-vessel *Guardian* could be seen on fire, with *Active* towing her clear. *Nelson* detailed off a hundred men as a fire party, and off went the motor-cutter with the Engineer Commander, Torpedo Officer and key ratings, with the diesel pump and portable foam generator. It was reported that a limpet charge had gone off on one of the 85-octane tanks. The fierceness of the blaze blistered the paint off the sides of the adjacent tank, which held 95,000 gallons of 100-octane fuel, and the petrol inside was so hot that one could not put a hand in it. Luckily, it did not ignite.

There were exercises at sea next day. After one day in harbour she sailed for Mers-el-Kebir, arriving at 0815 on 4 July flying a large Stars and Stripes at the main to mark Independence Day. The port was crammed with ships of all kinds including the American cruisers *Philadelphia*, *Brooklyn* and *Birmingham*.

At 1300 the following day she prepared for sea. A French tug got her tow wire round her own screw and her crew put up an apathetic performance. 'What they want is another Joan of Arc,' muttered Chief Petty Officer Sadler.

An hour later *Nelson* was steaming east. The invasion of Sicily – Operation 'Husky' – was just a few days away, when the Americans would land in the south of the island and the British in the south-east, with the dividing line between them at Cape Regilione. On 6 July, masses of shipping were on the move, taking up their allotted positions. Surely the

Italian fleet would at last come out to defend their homeland. Waiting for them in the Ionian Sea would be Force 'H' supplemented by the battleships *Valiant* and *Warspite*.

Next day, Force 'H' passed Cape Bon, rising 1,873 feet above sea level. The Polish destroyer *Piorun* was leading, then the cruiser *Cleopatra*, then *Nelson*, *Indomitable*, *Rodney*, the cruiser *Euryalus* and the rest of the destroyers on the flanks. The course was 165°, Pantelleria appeared hazily on the port beam at 1730, and during the night the Force passed between Lampedusa and Linosa. Early on 8 July they were south of Malta and some old friends of the 12th Destroyer Flotilla (*Laforey, Lookout, Loyal, Eskimo, Tartar* and *Nubian*) took over the screen while the Force 'H' destroyers went off to refuel. Later the cruisers *Aurora* and *Penelope* joined. At 1430 the flagship passed a despatch buoy to *Euryalus*, then she and *Cleopatra* went off to Tripoli to refuel. All the invasion convoys were now massing south of Malta and Sicily and just north of the Tripolitanian coast.

At 0600 on the 9th, the Second Division (*Valiant, Warspite* and the aircraft carrier *Formidable*) joined. Two oilers were expected at 0630, and when only one arrived the Admiral signalled, 'Battleships prepare to oil destroyers.' The gear was quickly rigged port side with the crane. *Eclipse* came alongside to take despatches to *Indomitable* which had an Albacore ticking over on the catapult, the papers were given to the Observer and she took off at once for Cyrenaica.

Captain Russell showed the Commander a disquieting signal which contained the gaffe, 'Troops on the beaches must cheerfully accept enemy air attack.' 'Cheerfully!' repeated the Captain, 'The man on the office stool might have left that word out.'

As the time for the invasion approached, the Force turned north and went up to eighteen knots, the four battleships in diamond or 'open' formation, the two aircraft carriers in extended order to starboard, and the destroyers spread in a great fan. It was blazing hot, the sea just gently ruffled and the sky cloudless. At about 1800 everybody went into battle rig, mainly overalls with trousers tucked into socks, and anti-flash gear handy. To beat the heat between decks, canvas chutes were rigged during the day down the heads and sick-bay flat hatches, and the decks were kept wet.

A snooper appeared at 1830 and the fleet went to first-degree AA readiness. At dusk the heavy ships went into line ahead. If the Italians hoped to thwart the landings, now was the time to strike. But the radar screens showed no unidentified ships, and at 2130 the fleet went down to second-degree High-Angle (that is, AA) readiness and third-degree Low-Angle and Damage Control readiness, and then at midnight to third-degree HA.

The wind had been steadily increasing and it was blowing Force 5 at midnight. Many philosophized that they were glad to be sailors and not soldiers, thinking of the unfortunates huddled in the landing-craft, covered with spray, feeling sea-sick and waiting to land on an unknown beach after a fortnight in a cramped, blazing hot transport.

Saturday, 10 July, was Invasion Day. At 0430 Force 'H' went to full Action Stations as it patrolled the Ionian Sea. There were no enemy reports, and no radar contacts, so after closing up and shutting all 'Y' armoured hatches and testing communications, there was an issue of cocoa. Brief reports started to come through. The Commandos had captured their beaches. Individual cruisers and destroyers were called upon to silence shore batteries which were annoying the invaders. Reports at 0630 said that most of the beaches were in our hands.

Daylight came and still there was no report of the enemy. On longitude 16°E, Force 'H' steamed up and down waiting for an adversary who never came. For the ship's company who had worked so hard to bring *Nelson* to a peak of fighting efficiency, it was disappointing and a great anticlimax.

It was in fact a perfect example of the proper use of sea power. We had chosen the time and place to bring a strong, well-trained fleet, which was now interposed between the Allied landings and the enemy's powerful naval forces; and the enemy had assessed our strength and his own chances of success. Without a shot being fired, the naval issue had been decided.

Nothing happened during the day except a few air alarms. At dusk, the ship went to first-degree HA for a time and then remained at second-degree until midnight. At 0430 on the 11th there was full Action Stations for about one and a half hours. When dawn came, Etna stood out clear 92 miles away, and the toe of Italy to the north. It was a beautiful golden morning, but when fifty Liberators flew overhead it was a blunt reminder that conflict was not far away. After another uneventful day, *Nelson* took her Division to Malta early on the 12th, leaving the Second Division on patrol.

On the way in, Admiral Ramsay passed in a destroyer and signalled 'What is that I see at your masthead – a broom?' *Nelson* anchored off the breakwater of Grand Harbour at 0915. Ricasoli Bay was crowded with landing-craft packed tight with guns and vehicles. Up to midnight on the 11th, 160,000 men, 12,000 vehicles and 700 tanks had been landed in Sicily.

At 1300 *Nelson* led her Division from Malta, passed the Second Division coming in to refuel, and overhauled a flotilla of huge LSTs on their way to the Sicilian port of Syracuse which the Allies had brought into use. The destroyer *Tartar* came in sight towing her sister ship, *Eskimo*, an early victim of the glider-bomb. Her back was broken and she had suffered 16 dead and 22 wounded.

Fruitless patrolling continued to occupy Force 'H' for the next few days. On Friday, 16 July, bursts of firing were heard at 0030, and shortly afterwards it was learned that the aircraft carrier *Indomitable* had been torpedoed. She was hit abreast the port boiler-room which flooded and gave her a 12½° list, but she regained her trim within fifteen minutes. *Nelson* escorted her back to Malta and *Formidable* took her place. A signal was received to go and bombard Catania and as the Force went north, Syracuse, Porco Murro and the hilly hinterland could be seen distinctly. But to everyone's disappointment the order for bombardment was cancelled.

That night the radar screens were very busy with unidentified aircraft. The ship was at first-degree most of the time, blazing away, with the guns controlled by radar barrage director. The splash of a torpedo and its track close to the ship were seen, but, apart from the streams of tracer, most of the activity was hidden by the darkness. During the morning of the 17th, the ship arrived at Malta and went up harbour at 0930.

The following Tuesday, 20 July, the enemy sent in thirty bombers at 0330. Men strove to furl the quarterdeck awning as the ship vibrated to the crack and chatter of the guns. The barrels of the starboard 4.7s became so hot that the paint peeled off in one piece like the bark of a tree. 'HA3' gun alone fired 83 rounds. For the next two nights the enemy tried again, but without success.

The ship's complement was now 1,756, and fresh water consumption 100 tons a day. One set of evaporators failed while the ship lay in Grand Harbour, making life rather difficult for everyone as the use of water had to be restricted.

On 26 July news came of Mussolini's resignation and of Marshal Badoglio's taking over in Italy. So the first of the great dictators was toppled, and there was speculation as to how much longer Italy would be in the war. By now the Royal Navy had complete mastery of all the supply routes through the Mediterranean; and Force 'H' enforced that mastery from its new Malta base.

On 23 August there was a big explosion at the bottom of the Barracca lift in Valletta. Many people were killed in what was thought to be the result of a delayed-action bomb from one of the many air raids. *Nelson* sent parties to help and clear away wreckage, but there was little they could do for the victims. Everyone expected the armies to move into southern Italy as soon as the occupation of Sicily was complete, and then Malta's long ordeal should be at an end.

For the present the island continued to endure. There was, however, one measure of help the fleet could give, as every big ship had an excellent bakery. When Force 'H' was in Grand Harbour it was baking 9,000 pounds of bread a day, and a substantial proportion of this was going ashore for the Maltese people. Before *Nelson* departed from Malta, the people of Valletta presented the Chief Cook with an illuminated address; it contained the parable of the loaves and the fishes.

On 27 August, *Nelson* and *Rodney* proceeded through the Comino Channel and did a number of exercises including a main and secondary armament shoot at the small, un-inhabited island of Filfla, south of Malta. Spotting aircraft co-operated with the battleships and the results were excellent.

If things went well on the 27th, they were just the reverse the next day. The ship entered Grand Harbour at 1700, did a beautiful turn, the cutter reached the buoy in record time, but in hauling back the grass line it parted. The tug *Restive* misinterpreted the situation and put her stern against the ship and pushed. In no time at all *Nelson*'s line was wrapped firmly around the tug's screw. The tug was now derelict between the flagship and the buoy and it was impossible to pass another line. *Nelson* worked her screws to correct the situation, but it was too late and she swung helplessly aground aft. Two of the ship's boats pushed against the port quarter and this helped to prevent the ship going on with any force. Next they pushed *Restive* clear, another line was passed to the buoy, they hauled back the second wire, brought it to the capstan and managed to pull the ship off and make fast. The diver was sent down and reported no damage to the screws or rudder.

The ship ammunitioned and generally cleared up the following day, and assistance was given to *Restive* to free her screw. At 1930 Force 'H' proceeded to sea for Operation 'Hammer', a bombardment in the Messina Straits.

At 0700 on 31 August, the fleet was off Syracuse and

110

steering north. The scenery of the east Sicilian coast was wonderful, and the whole of Etna could be seen. The only signs of war were the broken-down bridges all along the coast road. When past Taormina and opposite San Alessio Point on the Italian mainland, the Force turned to the northeast and entered the Messina Straits. The ship closed up at full Action Stations, and the 16-inch turrets trained to starboard.

Just as the bombardment was about to commence there was an air alarm and two Junkers Ju 88s appeared, but they thought better of coming within range of the guns and flew away.

At a range of 30,000 yards, *Nelson* and *Rodney* opened fire on the shore batteries to the north of Reggio Calabria. The cruisers and destroyers went closer inshore to add their fire-power and some Italian shells began to fall near them; but the batteries concerned were quickly silenced. The pilots of the aircraft spotting for the ships' bombardment kept up a running commentary and some of them became very excited in their enthusiasm for the accuracy of the shoot, especially when one ship scored a direct hit on an ammunition store.

Late in the day Force 'H' returned to Malta, and the flagship entered harbour and secured to her buoys in record time.

Before dawn on 3 September, the British Eighth Army began to cross the Messina Straits for the invasion of Italy. They encountered no opposition from the shore batteries and captured Reggio – the warships had done their job well. In naval command of the landings was Rear-Admiral McGrigor, and to encourage his men to move troops and stores across as rapidly as possible, he introduced a competitive spirit between the crews of the landing-craft so that the operation came to be called 'The Messina Straits Regatta'.

There was a conference on board *Nelson* the following Monday which gave all the signs of something brewing-up. It was one of the final planning meetings for Operation

'Avalanche', to put ashore at Salerno the US Fifth Army and the British X Corps. To give air cover and fighter protection on the beaches, the small aircraft carriers, *Battler*, *Hunter*, *Stalker* and *Unicorn* would operate inshore, and to protect the inshore carriers and the operation in general would be Force 'H' with the fleet carriers *Illustrious* and *Formidable*. The fleet sailed from Grand Harbour at 1600.

On Wednesday, 8 September, Force 'H' was in the Tyrrhenian Sea, an imposing force supplemented again by the battleships *Valiant* and *Warspite*, and including two French destroyers, *Fantasque* and *Terrible*. At 1835 the news of Italy's surrender came through and five minutes later the BBC confirmed it. The feeling that the Salerno landing would now be a walk-over was very quickly dispelled.

At 0300 on the 9th, the landings went in and the Germans reacted with ferocious energy. For the fleet it was a night of tremendous barrages against determined attacks. Some torpedo planes ordered to attack the troop transports came at the flagship instead (survivors from a Heinkel 111 picked up later from their rubber dinghies said that twenty to thirty planes in the first wave attacked *Nelson*) and one of them came close down the port side in a mass of flame. Noise, smoke and gun-flashes enveloped the ship, and the well-trained gunners followed their directors and kept up a fierce deadly rate of fire.

On *Nelson*'s beam, men in the aircraft carrier *Illustrious* had a grandstand view as the flagship fired everything she had, including her 16-inch. The intensity of the barrage shocked their senses of sight and hearing, and some of them said afterwards that their jaws and ears had ached from the battleship's tremendous gunfire.

The 4.7-inch gun was only partially automatic: the shell and fixed charge had to be fuze-set before being lifted up on to the loading tray, and the tray pushed over before the automatic rammer operated and the breech closed. A good gun's crew could fire a round every three seconds, and 300 rounds were fired during this night. The physical effort needed can well be imagined.

For those down below, in the Mediterranean heat and with ventilation shut off, conditions were appalling. The noise of battle could be heard above, but they were enclosed in their own small world with little knowledge of what was going on. One able seaman named Studley was in a 6-inch handing-room, receiving 6-inch cordite charges from the magazine below, and passing them up to the turret above. One after the other he placed the heavy charges in the slides to go up to the guns, for what must have seemed half a lifetime, and when finally the action was over and the 'Secure' sounded, he fainted from the heat and sheer exhaustion. While he had been needed in action he had somehow carried on. For the rest of his time in the ship everyone called him 'Cordite'.

During the day the Italian fleet was ordered to sea. *Valiant* and *Warspite* were detailed to escort the three *Littorio*-Class battleships from Spezia and Genoa, and *King George V* and *Howe* the *Cavour*s from Taranto.

When darkness came the German air attacks resumed and in six separate attacks Force 'H' was again heavily engaged. Once more the flagship put up her deadly umbrella of shells. A number of *Nelson*'s 6-inch and 4.7-inch gun barrels were now almost worn out and their replacement was becoming urgent.

It was not only the British ships which were under attack: the Germans turned in fury upon the Italian ships steaming to surrender and sent the brand-new battleship *Roma* to the bottom.

Throughout the 10th and 11th, the Force patrolled the Tyrrhenian Sea. On Sunday, 12 September, Force 'H' turned south and arrived off Malta in the dog watches. What a sight greeted them! Anchored off St George's were the Italian battleships *Andrea Doria* and *Caio Duilio*, three cruisers and a number of destroyers. *Howe*, *King George V* and *Warspite* were in 'B' anchorage off Ricasoli. Twice the lower signal-station told *Nelson* not to enter – a fleet carrier was across the harbour – the flagship lowered her boats and sent them on, and when all was clear she behaved impeccably and secured in Grand Harbour at 1830.

At 1130 next day, the Italian Commander-in-Chief, Admiral Oliva, arrived to pay his respects in a grubby boat and a boat's crew to match whose boat-hook drill was poor. He was received with formality, bugle and pipe, and although Admiral Willis shook hands it was without smiles.

On the 14th things were going badly at Salerno and the ship went to one hour's notice for sea. One hundred and eighty men from the USS *Savannah* came to a film show on board. Their ship had been struck by a glider-bomb on her 'B' turret.

During the night *Nelson* prepared for sea. A bright moon helped those getting the ship ready, and she sailed at 0400. *Valiant* and *Warspite* had been ordered to Salerno for bombardment to help restore the Allies' precarious position, and *Nelson* and *Rodney* were being brought forward to Augusta in Sicily.

At 1030 the two ships entered the fine big harbour at Augusta, with Etna a hazy pastel-blue to the north, and quaint, squat windmills working all along the foreshore. The ships remained at two hours' notice. The chart of Augusta was an Italian one and there was some amusement to find that if bearings of three objects on shore were taken to obtain a fix, which should result in the three lines crossing at a single point, the result was a large 'cocked hat' on the chart.

Ashore were many Allied service personnel. Hundreds of them were bathing in the sea and their shouts and laughter could be heard all over the harbour.

At 2000 on the 16th orders were received to leave at 2330 and return to Malta. The two older battleships *Valiant* and *Warspite* had done a superb job at Salerno, coming in to within a quarter of a mile of the beaches and pounding the German tanks and artillery at point-blank range. When the time came for *Nelson* and *Rodney* to leave Augusta a friendly moon again helped, the ships were off exactly on time, and in just over half an hour were down harbour and out through the boom.

During the passage to Malta, radar picked up an aircraft and the armament opened fire, but it was a friendly troop-carrier which had not identified itself. This was a continuing problem. All Allied combat aircraft were fitted with IFF gear (Identification Friend or Foe) but sometimes they did not switch it on, or there was a fault, or a wrong frequency was in use, and then their lack of identification made them very vulnerable.

The damaged *Warspite* was towed into Grand Harbour at 0900 on Sunday, 19 September, about five feet lower in the water and her radar mast awry. From a height of 23,000 feet a German aircraft had released a glider-bomb, which began its dive at 7,000–8,000 feet and went through three inches of *Warspite*'s armour and exploded in No 4 boiler-room. All the boiler-rooms, and all the starboard bulges flooded, 5,000 tons of water in all. Fortunately, there were only eleven casualties. Two of these were stripped to the waist, their overalls down, at a pom-pom mounting and were burned by flash from the boiler-room vents. It was one more lesson that the body must be kept covered in action.

Nelson was asked to supply *Warspite* with electricity. The flagship herself was beginning to have maintenance troubles, the cable-holder brake gear had to be stripped down, and the Commander and the Chief Bosun's Mate agreed that much needed to be done. They did what they could. Chief Petty Officer Sadler was firm in his belief that although many repairs were needed she could still look smart, especially if her masts and water-line were well painted. 'A smart woman always has a smart hat and a good pair of shoes,' he insisted.

On Wednesday, 29 September, the formal document for the surrender of Italy was signed on board. At 0800 the Italian cruiser *Scipione Africano* came in, a new ship looking prematurely old with rust in places. *Nelson* sent an Officer of the Guard to her. On board was Marshal Badoglio and senior officers accompanying him, including General Mason Macfarlane who was acting as British adviser.

The full pageantry was in the starboard waist. There was a full side with about twenty men in the piping party, Guard and Band. On the right of the Guard was a small but imposing group, brilliantly white in their uniforms, the unattached senior officers such as the Engineer Commander, the Paymaster and Principal Medical Officer. The Fo'c's'le Division was before No 3 break-water and stretching forward, the Topmen athwartships abaft No 3 break-water, the Royal Marines in the starboard wing and the Quarterdeckmen aft.

Admiral Cunningham and Vice-Admiral Willis left Customs House Steps at 0945 in *Nelson*'s barge. The ship bugled, piped and played *Rule Britannia*. At 0955 all the Allied Commanders-in-Chief came with their leader General Eisenhower, and five minutes later the Governor of Malta, Lord Gort, who received the musical salute *Garb of Old Gaul*. As the King's representative, he received ashore in Malta the National Anthem, but aboard *Nelson* he was regarded as on British soil where only the Royal Family were so entitled. After a pause a boat came from the Italian cruiser with Marshal Badoglio who looked very pale and worn.

He was courteously received, and after everyone had talked for a while in the waist, they moved aft to the quarterdeck and Badoglio, Eisenhower, Alexander and Cunningham went down to the Admiral's cabin. Finally, everyone went below, the formal signing took place, and the aides-de-camp and the secretaries to the politicians were entertained in the wardroom.

The actual agreement was unusual and was not simply a surrender: it has sometimes been called a document of cobelligerency. Shortly after this meeting, an order was sent to all Allied forces in the area in these terms:

Italy has been defeated and has surrendered unconditionally.

116

However, both the King and Marshal Badoglio have offered to help drive the Germans out of Italy and this offer has been accepted. This does not mean that Italy has become one of the Allied nations. Italians are ready to co-operate, however, and have been accorded the status of cobelligerents. Officers and men must be absolutely correct in their conduct. All demands must be through Italian Service or civil officials. Dealings should be conducted on a firm but courteous basis and as far as possible requirements must be obtained through the friendly co-operation of Italians. Where cases of non co-operation occur they are to be reported immediately to the Commander-in-Chief. Active resistance and hostile acts are to be dealt with as though committed by the enemy. Our present relations with the Italians are on an unusual basis and I rely on the tact and commonsense of all concerned.

When Badoglio and his staff had departed at about midday, the comment was made that he had been absolutely straight in his dealings with the Allies. After lunch, all the visitors were away by about 1330.

In Malta there was a serious water shortage. They had never known the rains to be so late or the sirocco (the hot southerly wind which blows across the Mediterranean) to stay so long. But the weather broke on 2 October, it rained in great torrents amid flashes of lightning, and the water poured down Crucifix Hill to Lascaris Wharf. The same day, *Nelson* sent a party to assist in mooring the Italian battleships. The *Giulio Cesare* had only one berthing wire in the whole ship, a rusty 2½-inch, and all her equipment was in a poor state. The ship's discipline, too, was bad and it would have been an absolute slaughter if such ships had attempted to fight Force 'H'.

And now it was time for Force 'H' to pass into history. While Britain had fought alone with slender resources against a triumphant Germany and a boastful Italy, there had been a particular requirement for a small, well-balanced task force based on Gibraltar to fight in the Mediterranean and to be available to sail through the Straits at short notice to add its strength in the Atlantic. To be able to say that one had served in Force 'H' was in itself a badge of honour. Admiral Willis left the ship at 0330 on Wednesday, 13 October, to become Commander-in-Chief, Levant, and Rear-Admiral Bisset arrived at 0900. But *Nelson*'s tour of duty as a flagship was almost over, and at sunset on Monday, 18 October, the Rear-Admiral's flag was hauled down with the ensign and she became a private ship.

The Trafalgar Dinner on the 21st was a celebratory affair, the King's Colour was brought up from the church, and the Captains of *Rodney* and the USS *Savannah* were invited.

Tuesday, 26 October, was departure day. At 0700 the wind went round seventeen points, the sky became filled with boiling grey clouds like a seething cauldron, and down came the rain. But spirits were high, and throughout the forenoon one could feel the ship getting on her toes. There is no mistaking the feel of a ship about to go to sea.

She got away perfectly at 1400, gliding out of Grand Harbour past the honey-coloured slopes of Fort Saint Elmo into the broad Mediterranean, did an HA practice shoot, and turned west for home.

Two days later the ship arrived at Algiers at 1030. Everyone was told that she would not be stopping at Gibraltar, and 600 liberty-men went ashore to buy gifts for their families. Next day the other watch had leave from 0900 and a similar number landed. She sailed at 1400.

On Saturday, 30 October, *Nelson* was south of Gibraltar at 2100 and passing through the Straits. It was always an eerie and wonderful feeling with Ceuta's lights to port, the shadowy Rock to starboard; Tarifa Point light on the starboard bow and Tangier's glimmering on the port bow – as if one were sneaking from one world to another. Paravanes were streamed for going through in case of enemy mines.

Next day, the Atlantic presented a grey, rolling sea, full of character. Men made their way to exposed watchkeeping positions in oilskins and sea-boots; and above the control tower, the air defence position described parabolas in the misty sky, making more difficult the job of the air look-outs.

Commander Alexander Matheson had arrived on board as relief for Commander Blundell before the ship left the Mediterranean, and Commander Blundell was effectively a passenger for the voyage home in the ship which had demanded so much from him over a period of nearly three years.

Five days later the ship was through the Minches and rounding Cape Wrath. She arrived at Rosyth on 6 November, welcomed with a huge pile of mail, and she prepared to begin her essential repairs at once. The first leave party left for their homes, but the ship could not yet expect a lengthy refit as heavy German units continued to pose a threat to our convoys, and *Nelson* was due to join the Second Battle Squadron at Scapa as quickly as possible. Captain Russell was appointed to the *Duke of York* and Captain Maxwell-Hyslop took his place.

In less than a month the ship prepared for sea, and she arrived at Scapa on 3 December escorted by the destroyers *Meteor* and *Opportune*. For the old hands there was the familiar routine of gunnery exercises and general drills in the Pentlands, and the newcomers soon adapted to the standards expected of them.

Duke of York was the Flagship, wearing the flag of the Commander-in-Chief, Admiral Fraser, and in mid December she left with the cruiser *Jamaica* and destroyers to cover an outward-bound convoy for Russia. On Christmas Day, *Nelson*'s mess-decks were cheerfully decorated and everyone enjoyed the traditional fare; and then during the evening word went round that the *Scharnhorst* and her destroyers were out, and this was followed by the order to raise steam and prepare for sea.

Events moved swiftly off the North Cape, however, and *Nelson* was too far away to play any part. The German ship twice tried to attack the convoy and was beaten off. Admiral Fraser was approaching at his maximum speed and at 1650 on Boxing Day starshell illuminated the target and *Duke of*

York opened fire in radar control at a range of 12,000 yards. Up to that moment the Germans were unaware of her presence; such was the superiority of the British radar. The *Scharnhorst* sank shortly after 1930 taking Rear-Admiral Bey with her; in the heavy seas only 36 of her company of 1,970 officers and men were saved.

The action altered the balance of sea power more strongly in Britain's favour. With *Scharnhorst* sunk and *Tirpitz* damaged by our midget submarines, the Admiralty were now able to reduce the forces based upon Scapa Flow and add more weight to the operations against Japan. It also eased the preparations for the invasion of France – the long-awaited second front – planned for the summer of 1944.

Nelson arrived in the Clyde on 12 January 1944 and during the next three months of training and exercises her ship's company came to know and appreciate the beauty of the Gareloch. Sadly, much of that beauty is now gone.

The ship's refit could not be postponed much longer, and she sailed from the Clyde on 30 March, arriving at Rosyth Dockyard on 1 April. The provisional date for completion was 17 May.

In the early months of 1944 southern England witnessed the gigantic build-up of huge armies, British, Canadian and American, which could only mean that a cross-Channel invasion was imminent. The Allied navies, too, were preparing for the mightiest invasion in history, and it was particularly fitting that Admiral Ramsay, who in 1940 was in charge of the Dunkirk evacuation which saved the British Army from destruction, should have been given the naval task of putting the Allied armies back on French soil.

It was to be an armada of more than 4,000 ships, plus several thousand more smaller craft, in which 79 per cent of the warships would be British and Commonwealth, 16 per cent American, and the remaining 5 per cent other European.

All over the country the tempo of activity increased and security grew tighter. *Nelson*'s refit was finished ahead of time and she joined the fleet at Scapa on 9 May. Now it only remained to bring her gunnery to a peak of efficiency. She was in the Clyde again from 18 to 24 May and was back at Scapa on the 26th.

As the various forces began to take up their positions for the invasion, *Nelson* left Scapa on 2 June and Captain Maxwell-Hyslop took her south to Milford Haven. The story of 6 June has been recounted many times. During the morning, the BBC told the people of Britain of the landings and, aboard *Nelson*, men listened incredulously and hilariously as an announcer said that the battleship *Nelson* was bombarding Normandy. At the time, her berth in Milford Haven could not have been more tranquil. It was an understandable mistake, but it was her look-alike sister *Rodney* who was hammering the Germans. *Nelson*'s turn came a few days later. She arrived at Portsmouth on the 9th and joined the bombarding squadron off the French coast on the 11th.

During the next seven days she fired nearly 1,000 rounds of 16-inch and 6-inch shell in twenty separate bombardments at extreme ranges.

The accuracy of these shoots astounded the Germans and reports which became available after the war testified to their effect. It was the partnership of air superiority and unhindered spotting aircraft, operating with a well worked-up battleship, that prevented the enemy from concentrating his troops effectively, and hounded them in retreat eighteen and a half miles inland with terrible and unerring destruction. Field Marshal Rommel reported to Hitler that operations were impossible within range of the heavy naval guns; the blast effect from a near miss by a 16-inch shell could flip over a German 45-ton Panther tank. Allied units ashore singled out *Nelson*'s gunnery for special praise, and there was particular mention of her bombardment of Noyers and enemy batteries at Houlgate on the 14th, and of her silencing a battery north of Le Havre on the 16th.

An account in the *Philadelphia Inquirer* recorded that,

speaking a month later at the Bellevue-Stratford Hotel in Philadelphia, the Second Gunnery Officer, Lieutenant-Commander E. H. Pratt, RNVR, commented,

> Our fire was pretty accurate, and you may recall how one shell from our big guns scored a direct hit on and wiped out an automobile filled with fleeing Jerry gunners, who were miles from the coast and unseen by us. It was another example of how well our plane-spotting Observers directed our aim. We also took time out to smash an anti-aircraft gun that was annoying our spotter on another occasion, then hit our target the next round.

He went on to tell his audience that the Luftwaffe made three night attacks on the *Nelson* and that some of the bombs came fairly close. 'It was the mines dropped by parachute that gave us most concern,' he said, 'because their direction of fall was so uncertain, and they took a long time in coming down'.

On 18 June the ship was proceeding at 16 knots when two ground mines in 15 fathoms, probably of acoustic type with a charge of about 1,500 pounds, exploded almost simultaneously, one about 50 yards to starboard abreast the bridge and the other farther forward under the bottom. Double-bottom tanks were damaged and the outer bottom plating corrugated from abreast 'A' turret to the fore end of the forward engine-room, particularly between the port and starboard second longitudinals. Forward of 'A' turret, the double-bottom compartments below the forward store-rooms were damaged, there was uncontrolled flooding in one rapid-flood compartment, and the remainder abreast the damage had slow, controlled flooding. Several double-bottom oil fuel tanks were damaged and made common. Extensive, but largely minor, shock damage affected the 16-inch fire control equipment, secondary armament directors, ADO sights, radar and gyro compasses. By great good fortune, there were no casualties.

Soon there was a 3° list to starboard resulting from the flooding of some wing compartments, and this was reduced to 1° by pumping out the rapid-flood compartments.

She set course for Spithead and anchored in Stokes Bay. Within twenty-four hours the ship's staff made her operationally fit, but permanent repairs to the damaged outer bottom were needed. It was decided to reduce her complement before proceeding to a dockyard and about half the ship's company were disembarked. She weighed anchor just before midday on the 22nd, ten minutes later she fired a few rounds of 4.7-inch shell at a high-flying aircraft, and soon afterwards was heading down channel with her destroyer escort creaming along on the flanks.

At 0500 on 24 June, she was off the Clyde where she joined Convoy UC27 for North America, thirty merchant ships escorted by American destroyer-escorts, and the British escort carriers *Arbiter* and *Smiter*. Convoy routine had its own particular disciplines, and the gash chute sentry made sure that no one disposed of left-over food or rubbish except at stated times. A convoy could not afford to leave a trail on the surface of the ocean as a possible clue for enemy submarines. All ships ditched their rubbish together, and the convoy then altered course.

All over the ship, home-made inclinometers to keep a check on the angle of list were a source of great interest. As if to insult the old lady further, in mid-Atlantic on 28 June, there was a middle watch collision with an American merchantman, the *Fort Fetterman*, just after the convoy had made an alteration of course. The bows of the *Fort Fetterman* came up against the battleship's port side amidships, but when daylight came there was little to be seen except that one of the large fairleads was displaced.

The majority of the ship's company looked forward eagerly to their first visit to the USA, and stories circulated of the experiences of other RN ships which had refitted in America. In one of these tales, the hospitable Americans discovered that a British minesweeper had no refrigerator in the wardroom pantry. They promptly organized a subscription and in no time at all a dockside crane was gently

123

lowering a brand-new Westinghouse refrigerator on to the upper deck. Unfortunately, a not very bright dockyard worker mistook it for an ammunition ready-use locker and, before anyone could stop him, he had welded it to the ship's deck.

5

Far East and Finale

On 4 July 1944, Independence Day, the coast of New Jersey appeared in the haze late in the forenoon. Moving south-west, the ship rounded Cape May and, at 1400, she anchored in Delaware Bay. Bathed in sunshine on the far side of the bay was the State of Delaware, lush green countryside shimmering in the summer heat.

She weighed at 0900 the following morning and proceeded up the Delaware River. At one point a large ferry-boat was about to cross, but waited for *Nelson* to go by; when its passengers saw a battleship approaching they began to cheer and shout, and continued to wave at the British sailors until the ship had passed.

New Jersey still lay to starboard. On the port hand Delaware gave place to Pennsylvania and soon Chester appeared, birthplace of the gallant *Ohio*, and suddenly the Malta convoys seemed an age away. Next came Little Tinicum Island and Philadelphia was just ahead. Because the Royal Marine Band had been sent ashore at Portsmouth, the ship's loudspeakers blared out a friendly greeting to our Allies with recordings of two current pop hits, the 'Pennsylvania Polka' and the 'Jersey Bounce'.

Both watches were fallen in for entering harbour. As the ship passed the mouth of the Schuylkill River the helm was put over to port, and as many hundreds of American sailors and civilians watched, she turned slowly into her berth at the League Island Navy Yard. She was surrounded by evidence of the massive US building programme: the battleship *Wisconsin* was nearing completion, also the battle-cruiser *Alaska*, the aircraft carrier *Antietam* and the cruiser *Wilkes*

125

Barre. Nearby, the British cruiser *Cleopatra* was having 40mm quads fitted and would soon be off to sea.

When leave was piped at about 1600, the non-duty watch streamed ashore in great numbers and caught the trolley cars outside the Navy Yard which dropped them at the corner of 13th and Market Streets in the centre of the city, or they changed at Snyder Avenue for the subway trains. The contrast between what they encountered here and life at home was enormous. In British towns the wearying effects of the war had brought a certain dullness: it was inevitable, for bomb-damaged buildings were everywhere, there was the constant nightly blackout, and in very many people's diets soya sausages and dehydrated potatoes were commonplace. But here in Philadelphia the variety of food and drink seemed endless; and on many street corners kiosks offered free doughnuts and coffee or Pepsi-Cola to the serviceman. And over it all twinkled the neon signs turning night into multi-coloured day.

Nelson entered dry-dock and repairs began at once. Captain Maxwell-Hyslop departed and for a time Commander Matheson was Acting Captain. Then Captain Clifford Caslon, who had led the Lofoten Islands raid, assumed command and, in introducing himself, said how it had always been his ambition that one day he would command *Nelson*.

As the work went ahead it was clear that the ship was being prepared to operate in the tropics. All over the ship the ventilation system was being improved; on every messdeck an iced-water machine was installed. The armoured director hood was removed, and in its place on the flat top of the upper conning tower, two sponsons were constructed to take US Mk.2 quadruple 40mm guns fitted with Mk.51 directors, eight guns in all; and two more quadruples with their directors were fitted each side of the funnel, port and starboard, so tight-packed with the other guns that when 'HA4' gun, a 4.7-inch, trained aft, its muzzle was about five feet from the trainer of No 44 Bofors, who could not wear

ear-pads as he had to be on his head-phones to the director.

On each side of the boat deck a gallery was built to take five 20mm Oerlikons. In all, 24 extra Oerlikons were fitted. Petty Officer Gunner's Mate 'Wally' Hammond went with a selected party to the School of Naval Gunnery at Norfolk, Virginia, to train on the American Mk.2 Bofors.

For a time the ship's company was accommodated ashore in the American naval barracks; and Lieutenant Richards arranged through the British Naval Liaison Officer in the Navy Yard for parties to go to a rest camp at Birdsboro, in the hills near Reading. This proved very popular, although there was a shock in store for the Captain's steward, Petty Officer Smart, who while swimming in the lake was bitten by a water snake. It was non-poisonous and the Petty Officer soon recovered.

The Americans also worked hard to rejuvenate the ship's engines. At 1600 on 10 December, she put to sea for steaming trials off Cape May and reached her original 23 knots. Well-satisfied with the results, she returned to Philadelphia at 1700 on the 12th.

Christmas came and the kindly Philadelphians were overwhelming in their hospitality. The news from Europe was encouraging and there was a feeling abroad that this might be the last Christmas of the war. There was a new, wistful little song in which the young Frank Sinatra urged everyone to have a merry little Christmas, and hazarded a guess that 'next year all our troubles will be out of sight'.

Her refit finished, *Nelson* slipped at 0930 on Sunday, 14 January 1945, went slowly astern from her berth, turned in the Delaware River, and headed for the sea. On the 15th the weather off the New Jersey coast was atrocious and no one was allowed on the upper deck. For a time an American tanker was just a few cables away, and it seemed as if she were below the wave-tops one moment, and the next moment, towering above.

The following day, the 16th, the ship arrived at New York at 1300 and occupied one of the Cunard berths at Pier 50 on

127

the Hudson River. The city was in the full grip of winter. She sailed again shortly after midday on the 18th in Convoy CU55, with ice two inches thick in places and snow piled up on the cable deck and on the 16-inch gun barrels.

As she stood out to sea the new 40mm guns' crews were exercised. All around, the ships of the convoy were pitching violently in the heavy weather, and the American destroyer escorts appeared to have a particularly lively time. Two days out the snow and ice had disappeared, and it was noticeably milder.

The return to the UK was relatively uneventful, German submarine activity was minimal at this time, but there was some depth-charging as the convoy entered the Western Approaches.

More dockyard work was necessary at Portsmouth, where she arrived at 1500 on 28 January, and there was intense activity on arrival as officers and men worked together for three days to deammunition ship, starting at 0600, with only half-hour breaks for meals, and piping down just before midnight. Then the ship entered C Lock in the dockyard and the first watch went on leave. If any proof were needed that *Nelson* was a happy ship it was amply illustrated by the numbers volunteering to serve in her as she was brought up to full complement. The additional armament needed about 100 extra gunners over and above the 1944 watch bill.

Nelson re-commissioned on 14 April 1945, and she was a very different ship from the 1939 Home Fleet Flagship. Instead of a handful of anti-aircraft guns, she mounted no less than 129 close-range weapons, and the personnel to man them formed the Close Range Gunnery Division. Their Divisional Officer, who was also the Air Defence Officer, was Lieutenant S. P. Pyke, RNVR, a solicitor in civilian life, and he was splendidly supported by the Assistant Air Defence Officer, Mr Durn, Gunner; by the Divisional Chief, Chief Petty Officer Buckland, and by a solid body of senior rates. The new Division very quickly developed its own *esprit*, and this became particularly evident in the field of sport. Most of the men were qualified AA gunnery rates, although a minority were seamen transferred from other Divisions.

Speed of action was the keynote of the Close Range Division, which was accommodated in two mess-decks port side of the main deck; that is, the deck immediately below the upper-deck. They were not allowed to go below main-deck level when the ship was at sea in an operational area. They had to be able to man their guns in seconds.

The air lookouts, high in the Air Defence Position above the control tower, were all qualified Oerlikon gunners, and there were always eighteen air lookouts on watch (six on the binoculars, six to read off bearing and angle of sight, and six 'stood down' in a nearby caboosh; and they changed round every twenty minutes). Thirty-six of the Oerlikon guns were colour-coded, half red and half blue. If the 'Alarm to Arms' sounded when the White Watch of air lookouts were on watch, the Red Watch air lookouts closed up on the red guns and the Blue Watch on the blue guns; but if the Blue Watch were in the Air Defence Position as lookouts, the Red Watch manned the red guns and the White Watch the blue guns. Non-watchkeepers manned the remaining Oerlikons. The whole organization was designed to save precious seconds; and the captains of watchkeeping pom-poms and Bofors expected to be ready to fire within about six seconds of an alarm.

With her increased complement, space was very limited. One oasis of quiet was the Church (or sometimes referred to as Chapel) of Saint Christopher, which was situated star-board side aft in the middle-deck cabin flat. It was fully panelled in light oak, and over the scuttles were roundels of oak enclosing stained glass. In harbour, when the deadlights and scuttles were opened, they were extremely beautiful. The ship carried three Chaplains: Anglican, Roman Catholic and Free Church.

At 0700 on Sunday, 29 April, *Nelson* left Spithead and immediately her work-up began. As she went down Channel the pom-poms were exercised in surface firings. It was a time for testing men and equipment, and very little was at fault. One factor was that after nearly six years of war some of the hostilities-only conscripts were middle-aged men. As the eight guns of 'M.3' pom-pom opened fire, a 44-year-old supply number crouched down behind the mounting, his nervous system quite unable to cope with the thunderous roar as each gun fired two shells per second, and other gun mountings nearby joined in. In no sense was it an expression of cowardice; it was simply that the unfortunate man was physically incapable of being a member of a gun's crew. This was an isolated case, but it was best to discover such things at the start.

At 1800 on 3 May the ship arrived at Gibraltar, collected mails, and sailed again at 2130, arriving at Malta on the 5th. She entered Grand Harbour, Valletta, at midday and berthed in Ricasoli Bay. A little way off the battered superstructure and funnel of the tanker *Ohio* remained silent sentinels above the waters of the bay. For many of the ship's company it was a kind of homecoming, and a reminder of difficult times.

Malta was to be *Nelson*'s base for the work-up and everything was laid on. The ship went to sea with *Anson* and the two battleships used each other as targets for main armament throw-off shoots. Parties of gunners went ashore to Fort Saint Elmo for Japanese aircraft recognition classes. The Allies had decided that involved titles like the Mitsubishi G4M, or Kawanishi NIK2-J Shiden, should be discarded, and that for recognition purposes boys' names should be given to Japanese fighters and seaplanes, and girls' names to the bombers and flying-boats. Soon, the silhouette cards of the Betty, Ruth and Oscar were as familiar to *Nelson*'s men as those of the German Ju.88 and Italian SM.79 had been in the recent past.

The Royal Naval Film Unit had produced an excellent training film in colour which showed a multiple close-range gun closing-up for action and then a series of attacks by enemy aircraft. As each man entered the cinema he was given a stick with a cartwheel sight at one end and a bead at the other, and now as the hostile aircraft approached on the screen he lined up his sight, estimated the target's speed and angle of approach, and allowed aim-off accordingly. About every four seconds a cartwheel appeared for an instant on the screen to indicate where one's sight should be. The value of this aid was undeniable, and subsequent shoots at sea proved the point.

There was a brief celebration of Victory in Europe on Thursday, 8 May. His Excellency the Governor of Malta, Sir Edmond Schreiber, gave a garden party at San Anton which was attended by over eleven hundred guests. The palace gardens were at their loveliest with bright patches of geraniums, bougainvillaea, roses, sweet peas and lilac, and the scent of the flowers mingled with that of the orange groves.

On board, a piano was hauled up on to the upper deck. As always, the accordion playing of Able Seaman Dave Lynn was in great demand.

The celebration had to be brief as the ship had a tight programme and was at sea most days, sometimes anchoring for the night in one of the bays at the eastern end of the island. Replenishment at sea was becoming a particular feature of exercises and the ship worked hard to perfect oiling destroyers and minesweepers alongside.

The work-up lasted about a month and on 12 June she was at sea for her final shoots. On board was Vice-Admiral (Malta) and Flag Officer, Central Mediterranean, Vice-Admiral Sir Frederick Dalrymple-Hamilton, KCB, to witness the standard of gunnery. The Gunnery Officer, Lieutenant Commander M. C. Creagh-Osborne, must have been well satisfied with the analysis of twelve 16-inch salvos which showed six direct hits and six straddles.

Perhaps the Air Defence Officer had mixed feelings about his close-range guns: though they destroyed the sleeve targets, some shells from M.6 pom-pom parted a signal halyard and a great mass of flags and pendants floated down over the guns' crews, causing very loud and widespread laughter. It was no one's fault. The training stops of all guns were set so that one could not fire at one's own super-structure, but this did not include running rigging.

Nelson sailed from Malta on 14 June, in company with *Anson* and the cruiser *Sussex*. *Anson* was on her way to join the British Pacific Fleet, and early on the 16th she proceeded independently to Port Said. As the other two approached Alexandria, there was the astonishing sight of mile after mile of ships, almost all of them merchantmen, which had not reached harbour, their rusting masts and funnels showing above water. It was an immense and depressing graveyard of once proud ships which had fallen victim to mine or torpedo, or to a sudden bombing attack. At 1600 the ship berthed. There were stores to be embarked, and everyone had the opportunity of shore leave.

She sailed again at 0600 on 21 June, and next day did a 16-inch and 6-inch bombardment on the range at Mersa Matruh. During the evening she turned east and set course for Port Said. On VE-Day censorship had been lifted, but an announcement was now made that censorship was again in force as the ship was about to enter the Japanese theatre of operations.

When the ship arrived at 1600 on the 23rd, the waterfront at Port Said was full of interest, handsome buildings, and animated tradesmen anxious to do business with the new arrivals.

Normally the ship was steered from below armour, many decks down, but for the passage through the Suez Canal visual steering was employed and the jackstaff and forestay were rigged. She began her passage of the Canal at 0700 the following morning. It was very hot and windscoops were fitted in all the open scuttles to draw a little air into the messes. At 1900 she anchored at Suez, an oiler came alongside, and 3,000 tons of fuel was pumped aboard.

On 27 June, she sailed at 1400 in company with the

cruisers *Sussex* and *Cleopatra*, and passed Mount Sinai in the early evening. Temperatures in the engine- and boiler-rooms became almost unbearable as she steamed south-east through the Red Sea, and for some periods watchkeepers were limited to a stint of not more than twenty minutes below. *Cleopatra* parted company during the 29th, carrying mails for Aden, and she re-joined on 1 July after the Force had cleared the Straits of Bab-el-Mandeb.

The weather was uncertain and the seas were rising as they entered the Indian Ocean, and by the following morning it was blowing fairly hard. It all combined to create one of the most beautiful pictures imaginable: the three taut ships in line abreast, newly-painted in their light-grey with dark-grey centre panels on the hull, quarterdeck awnings spread, dipping their bows into the bright blue, sparkling sea, and the masses of startling foam racing aft, whiter by far than any wash-day could achieve. Visibility was perfect, and every detail of the wonderful scene stood out bold and clear, a never-to-be-forgotten imprint on the mind.

For the next two days the ships plunged eastwards in heavy weather. All awnings had been furled and stowed, and during the night of the 3rd the lashings on *Nelson*'s main derrick loosened and the huge spar started to flail from side to side with every roll of the ship, knocking a loudspeaker off the back of the funnel like swatting a fly. The emergency party had the unenviable job of securing it.

By Thursday, 5 July, the seas were subsiding and the next day was calm, a bright blue sea and hazy horizon, with the flying fish skimming alongside inviting the knifing bows to play games with them. Colombo appeared out of the haze just after midday on the 7th, and the ship anchored at 1300 in the very crowded harbour. Next to her was the assault-carrier *Hunter*, one of the large number of aircraft carriers in the East Indies Fleet. Initially, all the small carriers constructed on merchant hulls had been called escort carriers, but as their numbers increased the true escort carrier for convoy work specialized in anti-submarine flying, while attached to the aggressive task forces a new breed, armed principally with fighter-bombers, came to be called assault carriers.

Three days later, *Nelson* reached the main fleet base at Trincomalee, a fine tree-fringed harbour where she was to relieve *Queen Elizabeth* as Flagship of the Third Battle Squadron. Vice-Admiral H. T. C. Walker transferred his flag on the 12th, and the fleet cheered *Queen Elizabeth* out of harbour when she left for home on the 14th.

In Ceylon (now Sri Lanka), the ship's company quickly settled down to the tropical routine. To prevent malaria, there was a daily issue of mepacrine tablets, a substitute for quinine, and after a time this caused the skin to assume a yellowish tinge.

It was a busy time. The ship stored and provisioned, the Commander-in-Chief, Admiral Sir Arthur Power, came on board to address the ship's company, and on Monday, 16 July, she left harbour for two days of exercises and firings. During one 6-inch shoot a Fleet Air Arm pilot flew his aircraft close down the ship's side and through the barrage. It was an unusual form of Russian roulette, but he got away with it. In off-duty hours a series of inter-Divisional deck hockey matches was being played in the starboard waist. Despite the heat, there was a great spirit of competition and every match was well supported and cheered on by spectators.

After one day in harbour, the ship put to sea as Flagship of Task Force 63 for Operation 'Livery'. In company were the cruiser *Sussex*, the assault carriers *Ameer* and *Empress*, five destroyers and seven minesweepers. The object of this particular operation was to sweep a channel through Japanese minefields in the North Malacca Strait in preparation for a full-scale invasion of the Malay peninsula, to attack targets on shore, and to draw to itself, and away from the British Fourteenth Army fighting south of Rangoon, some of the remaining Japanese air strength.

For nearly three days the Force steered east at cruising

stations before closing-up at second-degree of readiness to pass through the Sombreiro Channel in the Japanese-held Nicobar Islands during the dark hours of 22 July. Despite normal secrecy over the operation, 'Tokyo Rose' came on the Japanese radio to announce that a British Task Force was steaming east across the Bay of Bengal. On Monday 23rd, *Nelson* oiled the destroyer *Rotherham* and minesweeper *Punjab*. The following day, the task force was at Defence Stations as it neared the coast at 0515, and the two carriers let loose their first strikes.

Ameer was embarked with 24 Hellcats of 804 Squadron and one Walrus reconnaissance amphibian of 1700 Squadron, and *Empress* 20 Hellcats of 896 Squadron and one Walrus of 1700 Squadron. These two ships flew more than 150 sorties in three days, attacking communications and airfields at Sungei Patani, Bandau and Alor Star.

The minesweepers began their less spectacular but very vital task of clearing a channel. At 1630 the minesweeper *Squirrel* was suddenly blanketed from view by erupting columns of water and spray, and a moment later came the dull sound of the explosion as she was rent apart by a mine. The survivors, including many wounded, were picked up by two ships of her flotilla, *Pincher* and *Vestal*. Seven officers and 87 ratings were transferred to *Nelson* and the rest of the survivors to *Sussex*. Soon after he arrived on board, the Commanding Officer of the *Squirrel* offered to take his turn at watchkeeping duties; the following morning one of his young sub-lieutenants was buried at sea from the starboard side of the quarterdeck.

The operation continued as planned and on the second and third days great havoc was wrought on shore by the Hellcats, and by an 8-inch bombardment carried out by the cruiser *Sussex*. The Japanese retaliated with Sonia bombers used as suicide aircraft, the only occasion when kamikaze attacks were made in the Bay of Bengal. Six or seven times each day, radar gave warning of the approach of unidentified aircraft and the guns' crews raced to their posts.

In one attack, five Japanese aircraft attacked out of a squall and one was very close to *Ameer* before being spotted. Guns in *Ameer* and *Nelson* opened fire and the Sonia was hit and destroyed only some 500 feet from the unarmoured carrier. The two ships shared the kill, but many who were on *Nelson*'s upper deck were convinced that it was the accurate shooting by her No 41 Bofors which brought it down.

Just before dusk on the 26th, a Hellcat spotting for a bombardment by *Sussex* saw a number of Japanese aircraft coming in. The Hellcat pilot was unable to get into a firing position before two Sonias were diving on the cruiser. *Sussex* shot the first one to pieces, although it exploded alongside, scarring her quarter; the other made off and then dived on *Vestal*, scoring a direct and mortal hit.

On one occasion, one of *Nelson*'s Oerlikon gunners, who was also a ship's barber, heard the alarm, picked up his anti-flash gear, and doubled along the upper-deck towards his gun which was situated between two 4.7s, 'HA2' and 'HA4', on the port side. 'Sweeney' should have put on his anti-flash mask and gloves at once, but he was so intent on getting to his gun quickly that he made the mistake of carrying them in his hand. Unknown to him, the 4.7s were following the pointers of their HA director which was already tracking a Japanese aircraft about to cross the ship's bows from starboard to port. He dashed up the ladder to the 4.7-inch gun-deck as the kamikaze came into sight. At that instant the two 4.7s fired and the muzzle of 'HA4' gun, a 50-pounder, was just over his head. The effect was to remove his eyebrows and half his hair, and to frizzle the remainder. When 'Sweeney' went down to his mess after the action he doubtless expected sympathy, but the appearance of the ship's barber with his new hair-do sent his messmates falling about with laughter.

The 4.7s were using the new proximity-fuzed shell, and in one firing 'HA4' gun suffered a premature burst, the shell exploding just after leaving the muzzle and only a few feet from No 44 Bofors and its crew. Bits flew everywhere but luckily no one was killed. 'HA4' was manned by Royal Marines, and the seamen took great pleasure in ribbing them unmercifully about the accident, although the fault was not theirs.

Again, there were pitiful sights as the survivors of *Vestal* were brought on board the flagship, many of them badly burned. The Principal Medical Officer approached Commander Matheson to say that there were now so many wounded on board that he must take over another compartment adjacent to the sick-bay. The Commander immediately ordered the Forward Close Range Guns Crews Messdeck to be cleared and dispersed to other messes. These men had been watch and watch on their guns for more than three days and had had little sleep, but they moved their gear out and then went back to move the belongings of the other men who were on watch. What they did next was typical of the spirit of the *Nelson*. It would have been understandable if they had done nothing more, but, tired as they were, they fetched buckets of water, soap and disinfectant, and completely scrubbed out their mess-deck before it was used as a sick-bay. No one had ordered them to do so.

The task force remained vigilant. The minesweeper *Punjab* came alongside the flagship for oil, and there were more burials during the forenoon of the 27th. For the loss of two minesweepers, more than 36 Japanese aircraft had been destroyed and an immense amount of damage done to their installations and communications on shore; and a channel had been swept through the minefield in readiness for the next operation.

The Force turned to the west and on the 28th went into three watches.

The following Monday, Task Force 63 arrived at Trincomalee and *Nelson* passed the boom defence gate at 0830. As soon as she had berthed, the stretchers of the seriously wounded were slowly and carefully lowered by crane into boats alongside, and the rest of the survivors quickly followed them ashore. The forenoon was spent in clearing up and the flagship was soon back to normal.

A delightful way to spend an off-duty afternoon at Trincomalee was to take away the 14-foot sailing dinghy, drop anchor in one of the many little bays, dive over the side for a swim, and then sail her back to the ship.

The next two weeks were occupied with storing and ammunitioning ship, more exercises at sea, and at 2100 on 7 August there was an alert for a suspected midget submarine attack on the harbour. It proved to be a false alarm.

The news came through of the terrible atom bomb attacks on Japanese cities and on 15 August was VJ-Day, Victory over Japan. As darkness fell Trincomalee was ablaze with rockets and Very lights, mostly from the carriers. *Nelson* was illuminated by electric lights for the whole length of her upper deck, and the two 44-inch searchlights planted a V for Victory in the night sky. The time of relaxed celebration was not for everyone, and the two staff motor-boats which were part of the Admiral's staff organization were out all night delivering sailing orders to warships and merchantmen.

A rapid decision had been taken that to re-occupy the Malay peninsular the same organization would be used as had been planned for an amphibious assault in September 1945, the 'Zipper' Operation. The slower vessels began to get under way early on the 16th. For the flagship there was to be an important preliminary, Operation 'Jurist', for the re-occupation of Penang.

Nelson sailed on Friday, 17 August, still in war routine with the guns manned. In company were the assault-carriers *Hunter*, *Stalker*, *Attacker* (all three embarked with Seafires), *Shah* (with Seafires, Avengers and Hellcats); the cruisers *London*, *Ceylon*, *Nigeria*; the Infantry Landing Ships *Princess Beatrix* (to which most of *Nelson*'s Royal Marine Detachment had been transferred) and *Queen Emma*; and escorting destroyers. By the 20th the force was off the Nicobar Islands, but there was now a delay because, as the Admiral explained to the ship's company over the speakers, the Allies had agreed that the formal surrender of Japan would take place in Tokyo Bay before any regional surrender.

It was all rather frustrating but the interval of about a week was occupied in customary style. A concert party was organized in the recreation space; one of the numerous items was 'CPO Pemberton and his 'knickerbar' bride (AB Tucker) in comedy and song'. The high-spot was EM Hirst with his quite amazing impression of Carmen Miranda, the American singing actress who always wore a fantastic headdress piled high with imitation fruit and flowers. There was an exciting final to the deck hockey in which the Midshipmen eventually had to concede defeat to the Close Range Division, who also collected the overall trophy for Divisional sport. While the ships marked time at the Nicobars, a warning was given that men on the upper deck should be careful when their ship was close inshore, because the local population still made use of the blowpipe and poisoned dart.

To everyone's relief the ship got under way at 0830 on 27 August, and anchored twenty miles north of Penang at midday the following day. There the Japanese emissaries came on board to agree landing arrangements, and they signed undertakings that no Japanese attack would be made upon British forces. After three and a half years of frequently barbaric behaviour and their gross ill-treatment of prisoners of war, there was scant sympathy for the Japanese and the envoys were made to feel the ignominy of their position: they boarded *Nelson* by jumping ladder, climbing vertically up the ship's side.

The formal surrender on 2 September 1945, was a ceremonial occasion. The after port gangway, scrubbed white, was in position, and at the head of the gangway the ship's brass name-plate gleamed in the sunlight. News reporters and cameramen were everywhere. Some of the guns were still manned in case of some last-minute violation of the cease-fire, but all other arrangements were as normal for receiving a senior officer. Captain Caslon and the Chief of Staff, Captain Abbott, led Rear-Admiral Uozumi below to the Admiral's quarters where he signed the formal surrender document for Japan, sitting with his aides at the same table where two years earlier Marshal Badoglio had signed for Italy.

With the negotiations completed, troops started to go ashore and on Thursday, 6 September, the destroyers *Penn* and *Redoubt* landed further contingents for the Victory Parade at Penang. *Nelson* led the march past with her band and seven platoons drawn from the seaman and engine-room branches. All her Royal Marines were in the parade.

She weighed anchor at 0400 on the 8th and steamed down the Malacca Straits. This was originally to have been D-Day for Operation 'Zipper'. The French battleship *Richelieu* (attached to Third Battle Squadron) joined at midday and the remainder of the assault force during the afternoon, a vast concourse of ships moving south. Paravanes were streamed because of the risk of minefields. In the midst of this great assembly the ship threw a rare tantrum: one moment all was serene, and in the next few minutes she lost both paravanes, the low-power system failed, and with it the main gyro, steerage failed and she began to describe a circle. Two black balls were hoisted to advertise the predicament that she was 'not under command', and key officers and ratings hastened to put things right. In about half an hour the emergency was over.

After a brief stop at Port Swettenham on the 9th, she continued to Singapore where she anchored off at 0830 the following day. Admiral Lord Mountbatten accepted the surrender of South East Asia by General Itagaki at a ceremony ashore on the 12th and all ships were represented.

It was a mark of the ship's versatility that on arrival she arranged entertainment over Singapore Radio and put on the Royal Marine string and concert orchestras, and a seamen's swing quartet.

From Changi Gaol came the emaciated survivors of more

than three years of imprisonment and near starvation by the Japanese, almost all of them were British and Australian soldiers, to be welcomed on board *Nelson* and other ships in harbour. The sailors gave the prisoners of war their spare towels, tooth-brushes and other common necessities, which were items of luxury to the visitors. After darkness had fallen there was an unforgettable scene as the boats taking the POWs back to shore left *Nelson*'s side. Someone in one of the boats began to sing the familiar words, 'There'll always be an England, While there's a country lane . . .' Other voices took it up, 'Wherever there's a cottage small, beside a field of grain. . . .' Now all the ex-prisoners were singing, and singing with a controlled emotion, 'There'll always be an England, and England shall be free . . .' The boats were being lost to sight in the darkness now, but still over the water came the sound of their voices, 'If England means as much to you as England means to me'.

So ended *Nelson*'s war. She had steamed more than 135,000 miles, taken part in the major amphibious operations of the European theatre from Lofoten to Normandy, and fought in some of the bitterest convoy actions. She had been torpedoed and mined, she had been the target for countless bombing attacks, and yet through all this not a single man of her ship's company had been killed in action. Small wonder that those who served in her held her in such affection.

Many of the ships started to return home at once; the 21st Assault Carrier Squadron (*Hunter*, *Stalker*, *Attacker* and *Shah*) went out on the 13th, but for the flagship there was still work to be done.

She was still at Singapore on Sunday, 23 September, when at 1030 in the forenoon the Thanksgiving Service for the end of the war was held at Saint Andrew's Cathedral. In that beautiful, brilliantly white building, Admiral Lord Mountbatten and service personnel and civilians of many countries joined together. All the ships in harbour were represented.

141

Coming so soon after the harsh Japanese occupation, when even the Bishop of Singapore, Bishop Wilson, was for a time imprisoned at Changi and ill-treated, one rather expected a makeshift service. But the beautiful processional singing of the cathedral choir, mainly Chinese, set the scene for a memorable and moving occasion. Bishop Wilson later returned to this country and was the Bishop of Birmingham.

At noon on 30 September, *Nelson* proceeded from Singapore in calm weather and reached Trincomalee on Thursday, 4 October, entering harbour at 1800 to find it almost empty, a strangely depressing sight after all the purposeful activity of a few weeks before. She slipped at 1200 on the 7th and arrived at Colombo the following day, anchoring at 1300. Many of the ship's company went ashore to buy gifts for their families, and the liberty-boats returned laden with such things as finely made ebony trinket boxes and rosewood bowls supported on carved elephants.

The demobilization of war-time personnel was based upon an age and length of service group, and it was decided that *Nelson* should meet the battleship *Howe* at Kilindini, Mombasa, to adjust complement as *Nelson* was going home first. On Thursday, 11 October, there was the usual bustle of preparation for sea: the fleet carrier *Victorious* slipped at 1030 for a 26-knot passage home, *Nelson* hoisted in her boats and stowed her booms and gangways, and at 1830 she departed the East Indies Station, her commission and her Far East programme, and indeed the war itself, cut short by the atom bomb.

The voyage to East Africa provided the opportunity for King Neptune to visit the ship again, and on 16 October there was the preliminary exchange of signals. The Admiral assured Neptune that both innocents and constant dodgers would be brought before his Court at Two Bells of the Forenoon Watch on the 17th, and that all old seadogs would be available to assist in the execution of his watery commands. In a separate signal, he urged *Nelson* not to anger His Majesty by actually cutting the Line and leaving

142

two loose ends.

At 1900 speed was reduced in anticipation of the Herald's arrival and at 1920 a look-out reported, 'Line right ahead, Sir, Line right ahead.' The Captain ordered, 'Stop Both Engines,' and then went down to the upper deck to greet Dolphinus (played by Lieutenant (E) Walley) who had emerged from forward. Captain Caslon received from him the Royal Command for the ship's company to attend Court the following day.

By 0830 the next morning, a raised platform in the starboard waist was ready to receive the Royal couple, and in the port waist was a second stage alongside the Bath of Brine. At 0900 the procession came aft down the starboard side: first the Band in football jerseys and Bandmaster Challis sporting a Chinese coolie hat, the Guard apparently a mixture of Scottish Regiments and the Household Brigade, then the trumpeters and the policemen who took up positions each side of the ceremonial route. Next came the Barbers and Doctors in long white robes, displaying their razors and lather tubs and their pills and scalpels. Then the important members of the Court: the Chief Taster in spotless white carrying a large ladle, the Judge suitably and sombrely dressed and the Clerk of the Court and his Assistant carrying enormous pens, and Dolphinus now escorting some of the Ladies of the Court. Finally, to a magnificent fanfare of trumpets and policemen's whistles, King Neptune and his Consort Amphitrite appeared with Maids of Honour bearing her train; a truly royal sight, the King in a cloak of Royal Green, carrying Trident and Anchor; and the Queen, demurely at his side, with her long, sea-green, fish-embroidered train, a neat toque creation, and little else. Not surprisingly, she received many remarks from the onlookers. Underneath the royal garments were Chief Petty Officer Pemberton and Electrical Mechanic Hirst.

Neptune paused to inspect the Guard and received an Oceanic Salute of sea-shanties, and then mounted the

143

platform with the Queen and her Maids of Honour. To a fanfare the Court was opened.

Dolphinus announced Captain Caslon who welcomed Neptune, thanked him for his help during the war just ended, and asked to shake his scaly fin. The King, clearly affected by the expression of gratitude, replied,

I've only been too pleased to help
To make the Japs and Germans yelp,
And thanks I owe to all who in this ship
Have fought to free my Oceans from their grip.

The speeches and presentations followed. Neptune declared Vice-Admiral Walker to be a Freeman of the Sea and a Commander of the Old Salt Horse, and to Captain Caslon he said,

To Singapore from U.S.A.,
You've steamed the *Nelson* night and day;
And now once more across the Main
You take the ship back home again.
For these excursions you shall wear
The Southern Cross and Polar Star.

The Captain stepped forward to receive his unexpected medals. Others followed: the Chief of Staff, Commander Matheson, two of the RNVR officers who received bowler hats, and representatives of various departments. To Leading Stoker Nesbitt he declared,

For not polluting my Domain
With tasteless liquid from your drain,
You have with my especial thanks
The Order of the Empty Tanks.

Finally, the King indicated it was time to move to the Bath of Brine, when singly at first but in ever-increasing numbers the malefactors and novices heard their warrants read and sentences were passed. The Doctors inspected and treated them, the Barbers lathered and shaved them, and they were tipped into the bath and into the waiting paws of the Bears

144

who meted out the final punishment of ducking with animal enthusiasm. The Queen was seen to mediate in some less serious cases, particularly with one or two South Africans who were accused of being on the wrong side of the Line. The Police meanwhile were going round the ship to seek out dodgers and any who were unwilling to pay homage to Neptune.

The proceedings went on until another fanfare was followed by an announcement that it was time for the King to return to His Ocean Bed. The Royal pair, followed by the Court, were led forward and away to their depths.

After one more day at sea, the ship arrived at Kilindini at 0300 on 19 October and berthed alongside the wall. Drafting commenced during the day, some men going to *Howe*, which in exchange sent over those of her ship's company who were due for release from the service.

Nelson moved out into the stream on the 21st, and that evening the Trafalgar celebration assumed a unique importance. Captain Caslon circulated a Trafalgar Day memorandum, and he wrote of Nelson,

> This is the man whose life has been the standard and the example on which we have tried to base our conduct and training in the Navy ever since. This is the man to whose inspiration over the long years we owe the endurance through the dark days of this war . . . until at last we have come to victory.

He said he believed that

> . . . if every British man and woman who ever saw Nelson's Column in Trafalgar Square fully appreciated the significance of its being there, this late war would never have been fought at all because it would have been prevented.

and he ended,

> I hope that in the days to come, whenever you think of or see Trafalgar Square, you will remember what Sea Power means to our Country, and determine that the lesson shall never again be forgotten.

The ship sailed at 1600 on 22 October. It was flat calm, the sun beating down, and flying fish the only companions on the journey northwards to the Red Sea. She arrived at Suez at 1700 on 29 October, and the surface of the water at Port Taufiq was an extraordinary sight, being almost completely covered by purple jelly-fish. The passage through the Canal was in two stages: to Ismailia by 1600 the following day, and the final leg to Port Said on the 31st where she arrived at 1700.

For those due for immediate demobilization the feeling of anticipation was heightened as *Nelson* entered the Mediterranean. She left Port Said at 0700 on 1 November and the next day was distinctly colder, a calm sea and visibility fair. She entered Grand Harbour at Malta on the 5th, the water-boat came alongside and she embarked stores, and then commenced to paint ship. Doubtless this produced mixed feelings, but there were to be many at Portsmouth to see her return home, and for this special occasion the old lady was going to look her best.

She sailed again at 1600 on the 9th, stopped briefly at Gibraltar for stores on the 13th, and that evening passed through the Straits into the Atlantic. By Friday, 16 November, it was blowing half a gale, raining heavily, and cold; but uppermost in everyone's mind was the return to England the following day.

At 0840 she passed the Outer Spit Buoy and was alongside at Portsmouth to a cheering crowd at 1000. Drafting ashore began at once and one watch went on week-end leave. She was dry-docked, and then long leave started the following Friday. It was a time of farewells and for many a time for picking up the threads of civilian life once again.

The first leave party returned on 10 December, the other watch went off the following day to enjoy Christmas leave, and when they came back on the 27th the ship was berthed at South Railway Jetty, preparing for sea. She sailed early on the 29th, arriving in Portland Harbour at 1300.

It was very appropriate that at the beginning of 1946, the

first year of peace, *Nelson* was once again Flagship, Home Fleet, wearing the flag of the Commander-in-Chief, Admiral Sir Neville Syfret.

On 7 March 1946, she sailed from Portland for the spring cruise – the very phrase had about it the ring of peace-time routine. She had with her the 10th Cruiser Squadron: *Birmingham* (Rear-Admiral Cunninghame-Graham), *Bellona* and *Diadem*, and the destroyers *Myngs*, *Zest*, *Zephyr*, *Zambesi* and *Zenith*. Land-based aircraft made mock attacks on the fleet as it steamed south, the RAF Mosquitoes approaching in quick succession to fire rockets and cannon at towed targets. For the warships the main training value of the cruise lay in radar interception and plotting, and there was a night exercise in which *Nelson* escorted by two destroyers was attacked by the cruisers and the rest of the destroyers.

After a pleasant interlude at Gibraltar, the fleet entered the Tagus River early on Friday, 22 March, and at 0800 the ships saluted the Republic of Portugal. It was the first visit of a British naval squadron for more than seven years.

During the war, the deck above the 4.7-inch gun-deck had always been called by its peace-time title of saluting gun-deck or, alternatively, 3pdr gun-deck, and now the Oerlikons had been removed and the 3pdr saluting guns were back in position.

At Lisbon, the squadron berthed alongside at the modern Alcantara Dock. At 0930 Admiral Syfret called on the British Ambassador, and together they made a number of official calls, the final one at noon to President Salazar at Belem Palace. There were return calls in the afternoon, and at 2030 a banquet was given in the British Embassy attended by the President of the Republic and many of the ships' officers.

For the next few days there was a tight programme of visits and receptions, President Salazar came on board *Nelson*, there was a friendly football match at the National Stadium, and the Royal Marine Band played in the Estrela

Gardens.

The British sailors acquitted themselves superbly well, and in an unexpected situation. While the ships were open to visitors on Sunday, 24 March, and thousands crowded the Alcantara Dock area, a section of a mobile stairway collapsed, killing some and injuring others. As if they had been rehearsed for the event, men of *Nelson* threw a cordon round the scene of the accident and then widened the cordon to include the foot of the gangway, a rating closed up at the controls of a dockside crane and gently lifted the fallen structure, and the injured were quickly carried up the gangway to the ship's sick-bay. As a mark of sympathy, men from the ship later attended the funerals of some of those who died.

The squadron prepared for sea on the morning of 28 March, and there were many Portuguese waving from the shore as the ships moved down river at 1045.

Shortly after the spring cruise, the Commander-in-Chief, Home Fleet, transferred his flag to *King George V*, and *Nelson* began the last phase of her career, as a training ship for young seamen who joined the Service for a seven-year engagement followed by five years on the reserve. In August 1946, she became flagship of the Training Battle Squadron at Portland, which also included *Anson* and *Howe*, a role she was to fill for the rest of her active life.

Only rarely now did she proceed to sea: the country's financial position was grave and the watchword was economy. For a ship which had been so travelled in war, it was perhaps a little embarrassing that the local telephone directory now contained an entry: 'Wardroom, HMS *Nelson*', followed by a number.

During the long hot summers of 1946 and 1947, the three ships were open to visitors in Portland Harbour. There must be many people today who remember going in the old paddle-steamer *Embassy* from Weymouth to stand and gaze in awe at the massive gun turrets of one of the last of Britain's battleships, to climb the ladders up to the bridge, or simply to chat to the young seamen or their officers.

On 1 February 1947, *Nelson* took her squadron out and, with the Home Fleet Flagship, met the new battleship *Vanguard* steaming down channel with the Royal Family on board, at the start of their tour to South Africa. This was probably the last occasion when as many as five British battleships manoeuvred together at sea.

Two months later, with dense fog in Portland Harbour, the submarine *Sceptre* left her depot ship and ran straight into *Nelson*'s armour, port side amidships. Only the ship's outer plating was holed, but the submarine's bow was extensively damaged. A motor fishing vessel bringing back overnight libertymen would normally have been alongside at the point of impact. Because of the fog the MFV was late.

At the end of September 1947, she left Portland for her last voyage as a man o' war, her paying-off pendant streaming out lazily in the warm air of a sunny autumn day. She de-commissioned at Portsmouth and with her sister ship was sold in 1948 for scrapping to Thomas Ward, Ship-breakers, of Inverkeithing.

As she lay in the Firth of Forth awaiting the end, she was used as a target for bombing attacks by aircraft of the Fleet Air Arm. As experience for the pilots it was of limited value. It takes only a moment's thought to realise that the planes were not attacking a battleship: if they had been they would first have encountered her own fighter cover, aloft and ready, and if they had managed to break through, they would have found a moving target putting up a daunting wall of smoke and shell. As it was, they dropped their bombs on a deserted, mute hulk.

By 1950 the work of the shipbreakers was complete.

*   *   *

In the quiet of Burnham Thorpe, tranquil but for the cry of the sea-birds of the Norfolk coast, where Nelson's father was rector and the young Horatio spent his boyhood and learnt about the sea, one can see in the church a White Ensign which the battleship *Nelson* flew during the Second World War. Elsewhere, you may find a few other relics.

The rest is history.

Appendix I

BATTLE HONOURS AND NAVAL OPERATIONS AND CONVOYS IN WHICH H.M.S. *NELSON* TOOK PART

HMS *Nelson*'s Battle Honours

Malta Convoys 1941–2	Sicily 1943	Mediterranean 1943
North Africa 1942–3	Salerno 1943	Normandy 1944

Naval operations in which HMS *Nelson* took part

		Code Name	
Sept	1940	'DF'	Home Fleet action against shipping off Norwegian coast.
Mar	1941	'Claymore'	Lofoten Islands raid.
Mar	1941	'SN69'	Cover for minelaying operation between Faroes and Iceland.
July	1941	'Substance'	Passage of Convoy GM1 to Malta.
July/Aug	1941	'Style'	Diversionary attack on Alghero by Force 'H', and passage of cruisers to Malta.
Aug	1941	'Mincemeat'	Attack on Tempio, Sardinia.
Sept	1941	'Status II'	Ferrying aircraft for Malta.
Sept	1941	'Halberd'	Passage of Convoy WS11 to Malta.
Aug	1942	'Pedestal'	Passage of Convoy WS521S to Malta.
Nov	1942	'Torch'	Allied landings in North Africa.
July	1943	'Husky'	Allied landings in Sicily.
Aug	1943	'Hammer'	Bombardment in Messina Straits.
Sept	1943	'Avalanche'	Allied landings at Salerno.
June	1944	'Neptune'	Naval operations off Normandy.
July	1945	'Livery'	Action off Puket, Siam.
Aug	1945	'Jurist'	Occupation of Penang.
Sept	1945	'Zipper'	Occupation of western Malaya.

Other convoys in which HMS *Nelson* took part

Mar	1941	WS7	Troops for Africa via the Cape.
May	1941	SL75	From Sierra Leone.
May	1942	WS19P	Troops for Africa via the Cape.
June/July	1944	UC27	Clyde to North America.
Jan	1945	CU55	North America to Cherbourg and British ports.

Appendix II

ADMIRALS WHOSE FLAGS
WERE WORN BY H.M.S. *NELSON*

Oct	1927	– Apr	1929	Vice-Admiral Sir Hubert G. Brand, KCB, KCMG, KCVO.
Apr	1929	– May	1930	Admiral Sir A. Ernle M. Chatfield, KCB, KCMG, CVO.
May	1930	– Oct	1931	Admiral Sir Michael H. Hodges, KCB, CMG, MVO.
Oct	1931	– Sept	1933	Admiral Sir John D. Kelly, KCB.
Sept	1933	– Aug	1935	Admiral The Earl of Cork and Orrery, KCB.
Aug	1935	– Apr	1938	Admiral Sir Roger R. C. Backhouse, GCB, GCVO, CMG.
Apr	1938	– Jan	1940	Admiral Sir Charles M. Forbes, KCB, DSO.
Sept	1940	– Mar	1941	Admiral Sir John Tovey, CB, DSO.
July	1941	– Oct	1941	Vice-Admiral Sir James F. Somerville, GCB, GBE, DSO.
May	1942			Vice-Admiral A. T. B. Curteis, CB.
July	1942	– Oct	1942	Vice-Admiral E. N. Syfret, CB.
Nov	1942			Admiral of the Fleet Sir Andrew B. Cunningham, KT, OM, GCB, DSO.
Nov	1942	– Jan	1943	Vice-Admiral E. N. Syfret, CB.
Jan	1943	– Mar	1943	Rear-Admiral Sir Harold M. Burrough, KCB, KBE, DSO.
Mar	1943	– Oct	1943	Vice-Admiral Sir Algernon U. Willis, KBE, DSO.
Oct	1943			Rear-Admiral A. W. La T. Bisset.
July	1945	– Nov	1945	Vice-Admiral H. T. C. Walker, CB.
Nov	1945	– Apr	1946	Admiral Sir E. Neville Syfret, KCB, KBE.
Aug	1946	– May	1947	Rear-Admiral H. Hickling, CBE, DSO.

Appendix III
CAPTAINS OF H.M.S. *NELSON*

July	1927	– Dec	1928	Captain S. J. Meyrick
Dec	1928	– May	1930	Captain T. H. Binney, DSO.
May	1930	– Dec	1931	Captain F. B. Watson, DSO.
Dec	1931	– Sept	1933	Captain A. T. B. Curteis.
Sept	1933	– May	1934	Captain P. Macnamara.
May	1934	– Aug	1935	Captain A. U. Willis.
Aug	1935	– Dec	1937	Captain A. R. Dewar, ADC.
Dec	1937	– Apr	1938	Captain W. T. Makeig-Jones.
Apr	1938	– Apr	1939	Captain G. A. B. Hawkins, MVO, DSC.
Apr	1939	– July	1939	Captain C. A. L. Mansergh, DSC.
July	1939	– June	1941	Captain G. J. A. Miles.
June	1941	– Jan	1942	Captain T. H. Troubridge, DSO.
Mar	1942	– Feb	1943	Captain H. B. Jacomb, CBE.
Feb	1943	– Dec	1943	Captain *Hon.* G. H. E. Russell, CBE, DSO.
Dec	1943	– Sept	1944	Captain A. H. Maxwell-Hyslop, AM.
Nov	1944	– Oct	1946	Captain C. Caslon, CBE.
Oct	1946	– Oct	1947	Captain E. B. K. Stevens, DSO, DSC.

Index

GENERAL INDEX

Abbott, Captain E. G., 13, 140
Aden, 133
Aircraft:
  Albacore, 79, 106; Avenger, 138;
  Beaufort, 65; Blenheim, 49, 50;
  Fulmar, 43, 44, 49, 55, 56, 79;
  Hellcat, 135, 138; Hudson, 79;
  Hurricane, 18, 49, 79; Liberator,
  104, 108; Martlet, 79; Mosquito, 95,
  147; Seafire, 138; Spitfire, 18, 79,
  80, 81; Swordfish, 46, 47, 49; Walrus,
  18, 135;
  German
  Heinkel 111, 82, 112; Junkers 52, 48;
  Junkers 87, 83, 84; Junkers 88, 81,
  82, 90, 95, 111, 130;
  Italian
  Cant, 48; Fiat BR20, 53, 54; Savoia
  SM-79 II, 52, 130;
  Japanese
  Betty, 130; Oscar, 130; Ruth, 130;
  Sonia, 135, 136
Alamein, 77, 78, 89
Alexander, General Sir Harold, 116
Alexandria, 78, 132
Algeciras, 42
Alghero, 46
Algiers, 89, 93, 95, 100, 118
Alor Star, 135
Alterations and Additions:
  Dockyard and Refit
  1932–34 and 1937, 17; 1940, 22, 23;
  1941, 32, 33, 58, 59; 1941–42, 62, 63,
  65; 1942, 87; 1943, 103, 104, 119;
  1944, 120, 125, 126, 127; 1945,
  128
Armament, *see* Guns and Gunnery
Army, 18, 22, 25, 26, 88, 98, 102, 106,
  107, 109, 111, 120, 121, 134, 141
  British 8th Army, 111; British 14th
  Army, 134; British 10th Corps, 111;

U.S. 5th Army, 111
Augusta, 114, 115

Bab el Mandeb, Straits of, 133
Backhouse, Admiral Sir Roger, 18,
  Appendix 2
Badoglio, Marshal Pietro, 109, 116,
  117, 140
Balearic Islands, 46, 47, 48, 90
Bandau, 135
Battle honours, Appendix 1
Bay of Bengal, 135
Beardmore, Revd Harold, 40, 41
Belem Palace, 147
Bennett, Admiral, 92
Bey, Rear-Admiral, 120
Binney, Captain T. H., Appendix 2
Birdsboro, 127
Bisset, Rear Admiral La T., 118,
  Appendix 2
Blades, Stoker, 69
Blundell, Captain George C., 12,
  23–25, 30, 46, 52, 53–54, 58, 71, 72,
  73, 76, 82, 93, 94, 115, 119
Bock, Karl, 102
Brand, Vice-Admiral Sir Hubert, 17,
  Appendix 2
Brettesnes, 26
Bridgeman, Dame Caroline, 16
Broich, Major-General Von, 102
Buckland, Chief Petty Officer, 128
Buoys, fog and mooring, *see*
  seamanship, ship handling, etc.
Burrough, Rear-Admiral Sir Harold,
  76, 84, 85, 86, 97, 99, Appendix 2

Cagliari, 58
Cape Bon, 85, 106
Cape May, 125, 127
Cape Regilione, 105
Cape Spartel, 42, 79
Cape Town, 31, 33
Cape Trafalgar, 59, 79

Capp, Able Seaman E., 81
Carius, Carl, 102
Carless, Major G. P. (RM), 100
Carnheros Point, 42
Caslon, Captain Clifford, 14, 25, 126, 140, 143, 144, 145, Appendix 2
Casualties, *see* Medical
Catania, 108
Ceuta, 118
Ceylon, 134
Challis, Bandmaster (RM), 143
Changi Prison, 140, 142
Chatfield, Admiral Sir A. Ernle, Appendix 2
Chester, 125
Churchill, Winston, 20, 22, 77
Church of St. Christopher, 129
Close-Range Gunnery Division, 128, 129, 139
Clyde, 20, 21, 22, 41, 67, 87, 120, 121, 123
Collision situation, *see* Seamanship, ship handling, etc.
Colombo, 133, 142
Commando:
  No. 3, 25; No. 4, 26; No. 9, 88
Concert Parties, 31, 59, 102, 139
Convoy routines, 37, 67, 68, 69, 70, 82, 83, 123
Convoys:
  WS7, 29–32; SL75, SL76, 36, 36–37; GM1, 41–44; WS11X, 51–56; WS19P, 67–70; WS5 21S, 76–87; UC27, 123; CU55, 128; WS20, 71,
Copenhagen, 17
Cork and Orrery, Admiral The Earl of, Appendix 2
Cowburn, Lieutenant-Commander G. G., 14
Creagh-Osborne, Lieutenant-Commander M. C., 131
Crossing the Line ceremonies, 30, 31, 35, 70, 142, 143, 144, 145
Cunningham, Admiral of the Fleet Sir Andrew, 57, 60, 89, 93, 100, 101, 116, Appendix 2
Cunninghame-Graham, Rear-Admiral, 147
Curteis, Vice-Admiral A. T. B., 51, 55, 67, Appendix 2
Cyrenaica, 106

Dalrymple-Hamilton, Vice-Admiral Sir Frederick, 131

Damage, *see* mines and torpedoes
Damage Control, 24, 53, 54, 56, 57, 67, 73, 76, 77
Darlan, Admiral, 90, 93
Davies, Leading Seaman Derek, 14
Delaware Bay, River, and State, 125, 127
Dewar, Captain A. R., Appendix 2
Durban, 32, 33
Durn, Mr. E. G. V., Gunner, 128

Eisenhower, General D., 89, 100, 101, 116
Emergency procedure, 74
Etna, Mount, 108, 111, 114
Europa Point, 42, 51

Ferrini, Tenente di Vascello R., 85
Filfla, 110
Findlay, Sergeant, RCAF, 50
Forbes, Admiral Sir Charles, 19, 21, 22, 23, Appendix 2
Forth, Firth of, 62, 65, 149
Fort Saint Elmo, 118, 130
Foster, Major, 102
France, 18, 22, 89, 90
  Invasion of, 120, 121, 122
Franco, General, 49
Fraser Admiral Sir Bruce, 119
Fredenhall, General, 92
Freetown, 30, 36, 69, 71

Galita Island, 43, 47
Gareloch, 120
Genoa, 113
Gibraltar, 17, 42, 45, 47, 48, 49, 50, 56, 57, 59, 60, 79, 81, 85, 86, 89, 90, 91, 94, 95, 96, 98, 99, 100, 101, 105, 117, 118, 130, 146, 147
  Ceremony of the Keys, 59; Italian underwater attacks on, 50, 91, 102, 105
Gloucester, Duke of, 59
Gort, Field Marshal Lord, 59, 100, 116
Greenock, 41, 67, 87
Gretton, Lieutenant-Commander J. H., 71
Grip Light, 23
Guns and Gunnery, 19, 20, 22, 24, 26, 38, 41, 43, 48, 50, 52, 53, 54, 55, 65, 68, 71, 75, 81, 82, 83, 87, 88, 90, 95, 96, 100, 103, 104, 109, 110, 111, 112, 113, 115, 118, 119, 120, 121, 122, 123, 128, 129, 130, 131, 132, 134, 135, 136, 137

Night Action encounter drill, 48, 68, 71, 88; Sub-calibre firing, 24; Throw-off firing, 34, 71, 87, 130; 16in main armament, 13, 15, 16, 24, 34, 35, 41, 48, 71, 82, 83, 87, 88, 104, 110, 111, 112, 121, 130, 131, 132; 6in secondary armament, 24, 34, 38, 53, 71, 87, 88, 110, 113, 121, 132, 134; 4.7in tertiary armament, 19, 20, 22, 24, 53, 68, 75, 81, 87, 96, 109, 112, 113, 118, 123, 136, 137; 40mm Bofors, 126, 127, 128, 129, 136; 2pdr Pom-Poms, 16, 20, 22, 65, 83, 90, 100, 130, 131; 20mm Oerlikons, 65, 80, 103, 127, 129, 136, 147; Multiple machine-guns, 17, 20; 3pdr saluting guns, 147

Haberkost, Leutnant Johannes, 21
Hammond, Petty Officer Gunner's Mate, 127
Harrison, Mr. W. S., Gunner (T), 52
Hatston Air Station, 23
Haustholm, 19
Havilland, Colonel Peter de, 102
Hawkins, Captain G. A. B., Appendix 2
Haydon, Brigadier J. C., 25
Henningsvaer, 25
Henson, Leslie, 102
Hickling, Rear-Admiral H., Appendix 2
Hill, Captain D. C., 70, 71, 72
Hirst, Electrical Mechanic, 139, 143
Hitler, Adolf, 121
Hodges, Admiral Sir Michael, Appendix 2
Hoffman, Victor, 102
Houghton, Surgeon Lieutenant P., 97
Houlgate, bombardment of, 121
Human torpedoes/midget submarines, 50, 90, 91, 100, 102, 105, 138

Iachino, Admiral, 52, 55
Ibiza, 46, 49
IFF (Identification Friend or Foe), 115
Indian Ocean, 133
Ionian Sea, 106, 107
Ismailia, 146
Itagaki, General, 140
Italy, 22, 109, 111
surrender of, 112, 113, 114, 115, 116, 117

Jacomb, Captain H. B., 65, 71, 86, 98, Appendix 2

James, Admiral Sir William, 102
Jamestown, 34
Japan, 15, 63, 120, 138, 139
surrender of Penang, 138, 139, 140
surrender of South-East Asia, 140

Kamikaze attacks, 135, 136
Kelly, Admiral Sir John D., Appendix 2
Kestrel HMS, RN Air Station, 20
Kilindini, 142, 145

Lagos, 67
Lampedusa, 106
League Island Navy Yard, 125
Le Havre, bombardment north of, 121
Leigh, Vivien, 102
Liebenstein, Major-General Von, 102, 103
Lillie, Beatrice, 102
Lindemann, Professor F. A., 22
Linosa, 106
Lisbon, 147
Little Tinicum Island, 125
Loch Ewe, 20, 21
Lofoten Islands, 25, 26, 126
Lookouts, air, 119, 129
Luqa Air Station, 50
Lynn, Able Seaman D., 131

Macfarlane, General Mason, 116
Mackilligan, Midshipman W. H. M., 94
Macnamara, Captain P., Appendix 2
McGrigor, Rear-Admiral R., 111
Majorca, 49
Makeig-Jones, Captain W. T., Appendix 2
Malacca Strait, 134, 140
Malay Peninsula, 134, 138
Malta, 17, 42, 43, 44, 45, 46, 47, 49, 50, 51, 60, 77, 78, 79, 80, 81, 86, 87, 106, 108, 109, 110, 111, 113, 114, 115, 116, 117, 130, 131, 132, 146
Manners, Vice-Commodore Errol, 29
Mansergh, Captain C. A. L., Appendix 2
Maps, Appendix 3
Marr, Paymaster Sub-Lieutenant J. A., 36
Marsaxlokk, 78
Marschall, Vice-Admiral Wilhelm, 21
Mason, Captain Dudley, 86
Matheson, Commander Alexander, 14, 119, 126, 137, 144
Maxwell-Hyslop, Captain A. H., 119,

121, 126, Appendix 2

Medical, sick bay, etc., 17, 21, 34, 69, 77, 96, 97, 103, 135, 137, 148

Mepacrine, 134

Mersa Matruh, 132

Mers-el-Kebir, 90, 91, 92, 96, 98, 100, 105

Messina Straits, 110, 111

Meyrick, Captain S. J., 16, Appendix 2

Midway, 78

Miles, Captain G. J. A., 24, 32, 40, Appendix 2

Milford Haven, 121

Mines, 21, 23
  Mine damage to *Nelson*, 21, 22, 122, 123

Minorca, 48

Modifications, *see* Alterations and additions, dockyard and refit

Mombasa, 142

Moore, Sergeant (RM), 30

Mountbatten, Admiral Lord, 140, 141

Mussolini, Benito, 109

National Day of Prayer for Royal and Merchant Navies, 74

Nelson, Electrical Artificer, 30

Nelson, Horatio, 19, 59, 149

Nesbitt, Leading Stoker, 144

New Jersey, 125, 127

New York, 127, 128

Nicobar Islands, 135, 138, 139

Normandy Invasion of, 120, 121, 122, 123, 141

North Cape, 119

Noyers, bombardment of, 121

Oliva, Admiral, 114

Omartak, General Saleh, 100

Operations, Naval, list of, Appendix 1

Oran, 89, 96

Oslo, 17

Panama Canal, 17

Pantelleria, 44, 47, 51, 106

Paravane, 61, 118, 140

Pemberton, Chief Petty Officer B., 139, 143

Penang, 138, 139, 140

Pennsylvania, 125

Pentland Firth, 67

Philadelphia, 125, 126, 127

Plymouth, 103

Portland, 18, 146, 147, 148, 149

Port Said, 132, 146

Portsmouth, 16, 17, 22, 121, 128, 146, 149

Port Swettenham, 140

Port Taufiq, 146

Portugal, 147, 148

Pound, Admiral Sir Dudley, 20

Power, Admiral Sir Arthur, 134

Pratt, Lieutenant-Commander E. H., 122

Prisoners of war:
  British, 140, 141
  German, 102, 103
  Italian, 87

Puccini, Tenente di Vascello S., 85

Pyke, Lieutenant S. P., 128

Radar, 18, 22, 62, 68, 104, 107, 109, 115, 120

Ramsay, Admiral Sir Bertram, 108, 120

Rangoon, 134

Red Sea, 133, 146

Reggio Calabria, bombardment of, 110, 111

Rescue of survivors from:
  HMS *Eagle*, 81
  HMS *Squirrel*, 135
  HMS *Vestal*, 136, 137
  SS *Cortona*, 75
  SS *Fofo*, 17
  SS *Strathallan*, 92

Richards, Lieutenant S., 95, 96, 127

Rommel, Field Marshal E., 121

Rosyth, 20, 62, 87, 119, 120

Royal Air Force, 18, 22, 49, 67

Royal Marines, 13, 137, 138, 140, 147, 148

Russell, Captain the Hon. Guy, 98, 106, 119, Appendix 2

Sadler, Chief Petty Officer (Chief Bosun's Mate), 70, 76, 77, 88, 91, 105, 115

St Helena, 34, 35

Salazar, President, 147

Salerno, 112, 113, 114

San Alessio Point, 111

San Anton Palace, 131

Sardinia, 48, 51, 55

Scapa Flow, 19, 20, 23, 24, 26, 27, 39, 41, 62, 65, 75, 76, 87, 104, 119, 120, 121

Schnerrenberger, Major-General, 102

Schreiber, Sir Edmond, 131

Schuylkill, River, 125

157

Seamanship, ship handling, etc.,
  Bad anchorage at Mers-el-Kebir, 92, 93, 98, 99
  Cable party casualties, 33, 34
  Collision situations:
    Near collision entering Durban, 32
    Near collision with unknown merchantman, 60, 61
    Near collision with aircraft carrier *Argus*, 67, 68
    Near collision with hospital ship *Newfoundland*, 91
    Collision with SS *Fort Fetterman*, 123
    Collision with submarine *Sceptre*, 149
  Fog buoy, 67, 87
  Grounding of *Leinster*, 42, 45
  Grounding on Hamilton Bank, 17, 18
  Inaccurate Italian chart, 114
  Main derrick, 95, 96, 133
  Mooring buoys, 65, 66, 110
  'Not under command', 140
  Ships boats:
    1st Motor-boat, loss of by fire, 73, 74
    2nd Motor-boat, recovery of, 72
Sounding by hand lead and line, 14
Sicily, 105, 106, 107, 108, 109
Sick Bay, *see* medical
Sinai, Mount, 133
Singapore, 140, 141, 142
  St. Andrew's Cathedral, 141, 142
Skerki Channel, 42
Smart, Petty Officer Steward, 127
Smuts, General Jan Christian, 32
Sogne Fjord, 23
Sombreiro Channel, 135
Somerville, Vice-Admiral Sir James, 42, 44, 45, 46, 47, 49, 51, 55, 57, 60, 72, Appendix 2
Southcott, Mr. H. A. (Commissioned Bosun), 14
Spezia, 97, 113
Sponeck, Leutnant-General Von, 102
Sport and Regattas, 35, 36, 37, 39, 41, 50, 75, 97, 98, 134, 138, 139, 147
Sri Lanka, 134
Stadlandet, 21
Stalingrad, 77
Stamsund, 26
Stevens, Captain E. B. K., Appendix 2
Stockholm, 17
Stokes Bay, 123
Studley, Able Seaman H. E., 113

Suez, 132, 146
Sungei Patani, 135
Surrender:
  of Italy, 112, 113, 114, 115, 116, 117
  of Penang, 138, 139, 140
  of South-East Asia, 140
Svolvaer, 26
Syfret, Admiral Sir E. Neville, 72, 73, 75, 80, 81, 84, 85, 86, 89, 90, 96, 97, 147, Appendix 2
Syracuse, 108, 109, 110

Tagus, River, 147
Tangier, 118
Taormina, 111
Ta'Qali Air Station, 50
Taranto, 113
Tarifa, 42, 118
Tempio, 48
Thanksgiving Service, 141, 142
Thornton, Petty Officer Diver, 93
'Tokyo Rose', 135
Torlesse, Captain A. D., 18
Torpedoes, 24, 25, 58, 59
  Torpedo damage to *Nelson*, 52, 53, 54, 55, 56, 57, 58, 59
Tovey, Admiral Sir John, 23, 27, Appendix 2
Trafalgar, Cape, 59
Trafalgar Celebrations, 59, 118, 145
Trincomalee, 134, 137, 138, 142
Tripoli, 106
Troubridge, Captain T. H., 40, 41, 46, 59, 61, Appendix 2
Tucker, Able Seaman, 139
Tyrrhenian Sea, 112, 113

Unrotated Projectile Mountings, 22, 65
Uozumi, Rear-Admiral, 140

Valencia, 49
Valletta, 109, 110, 130
VE Day, 131
Vernon, HMS, torpedo and mining establishment, 21
Vest Fjord, 25
VJ Day, 138

Walker, Vice-Admiral H. T. C., 13, 134, 144, Appendix 2
Walley, Lieutenant (E) L. G., 143
Washington Conference, the, 15
Watson, Captain F. B., Appendix 2
Wavell, General, 22
West Indies, 17

Whalley, Sub-Lieutenant J. B., 93
Willis, Vice-Admiral Sir Algernon, 99,
101, 102, 104, 114, 116, 118, Appendix
2
Wilson, Bishop, 142
Windscoops, 132
Wrens, 103

Yorke, Able Seaman, 70

Zahn, Leutnant Wilhelm, 20

INDEX OF WARSHIPS

Aircraft carriers: *Admiral Scheer*
(Ger), 23; *Ameer*, 134, 135, 136;
Antietam (US), 125; *Arbiter*, 123;
Argus, 41, 59, 60, 67, 68, 79, 87; *Ark
Royal*, 19, 20, 36, 42, 43, 44, 46, 47,
48, 49, 50, 51, 52, 54, 55, 57, 60, 73;
Attacker, 138, 141; *Battler*, 112;
Eagle, 33, 34, 35, 79, 81, 84, 87;
Empress, 134, 135; *Formidable*, 87,
88, 90, 95, 96, 100, 106, 108, 112;
Furious, 23, 41, 49, 50, 79, 80, 81, 87,
90, 91; *Hunter*, 112, 133, 138, 141;
Illustrious, 88, 112; *Indomitable*, 79,
82, 83, 84, 85, 104, 106, 108; *Shah*,
138, 141; *Smiter*, 123; *Stalker*, 112,
138, 141; *Unicorn*, 112; *Victorious*,
38, 39, 65, 79, 81, 82, 84, 85, 87, 142;
Wasp, 65
Battleships: *Andrea Doria* (Ital), 113;
Anson, 88, 130, 132, 148; *Bismarck*
(Ger), 36, 39; *Caio Duilio* (Ital), 113;
Duke of York, 62, 88, 89, 119, 120;
Giulio Cesare (Ital), 117; *Howe*, 88,
102, 113, 142, 145, 148; *King George
V*, 19, 25, 27, 39, 40, 65, 67, 88, 113,
148; *Malaya*, 26, 60, 67, 71; *Prince of
Wales*, 13, 39, 50, 51, 52, 55, 57, 63;
Queen Elizabeth, 19, 26, 27, 134;
Ramillies, 19, 23; *Resolution*, 62;
Revenge, 29; *Richelieu*, 140; *Rodney*,
15, 19, 20, 21, 22, 23, 25, 39, 50, 51,
52, 55, 56, 57, 59, 60, 69, 70, 74, 76,
81, 82, 84, 85, 87, 90, 100, 101, 103,
104, 106, 110, 111, 114, 115, 118, 121;
Roma (Ital), 113; *Royal Oak*, 19;
Royal Sovereign, 19, 41; *Tirpitz*
(Ger), 120; *Valiant*, 104, 106, 112,
113, 114; *Vanguard*, 149; *Vittorio
Veneto* (Ital), 52; *Warspite*, 104, 106,
112, 113, 114, 115; *Washington* (US),
65; *Wisconsin* (US), 125

Battlecruisers: *Alaska* (US), 125;
Gneisenau (Ger), 20, 21, 23, 26;
Hood, 19, 20, 26, 35–36, 39; *Renown*,
19, 42, 44, 45, 46, 62, 88, 89; *Repulse*,
13, 19, 63; *Scharnhorst* (Ger), 21, 23,
26, 119, 120
Cruisers: *Arethusa*, 23, 41, 42, 43, 46;
Argonaut, 88; *Aurora*, 106; *Bellona*,
147; *Birmingham*, 147; *Birmingham*
(US), 105; *Brooklyn* (US), 105;
Cairo, 85; *Ceylon*, 138; *Charybdis*,
80, 84, 85; *Cleopatra*, 106, 126, 133;
Danae, 74; *Devonshire*, 39; *Diadem*,
147; *Edinburgh*, 25, 29, 43, 51;
Euryalus, 51, 106; *Hawkins*, 33;
Hermione, 42, 43, 45, 46, 47, 48, 49,
51, 60; *Jamaica*, 119; *Kent*, 23, 24,
73; *Kenya*, 51, 65, 76, 85, 87; *Köln*
(Ger), 20, 21; *Leipzig* (Ger), 21;
London, 138; *Manchester*, 39, 41, 42,
43, 45, 85, 87; *Neptune*, 38, 39;
Newcastle, 31; *Nigeria*, 25, 26, 39, 76,
85, 138; *Norfolk*, 36; *Penelope*, 106;
Philadelphia (US), 105; *Phoebe*, 84;
Savannah (US), 114, 118; *Scipione
Africano* (Ital), 115; *Scylla*, 84;
Sheffield, 51; *Sussex*, 132, 133, 134,
135, 136; *Tuscaloosa* (US), 65;
Wichita (US), 65; *Wilkes Barre* (US),
125–126
Armed merchant cruisers: *Cathay*, 37;
Queen of Bermuda, 34; *Rawalpindi*,
21
Destroyers: *Active*, 105; *Antelope*, 39;
Ashanti, 85, 98, 99; *Bedouin*, 25;
Boreas, 35; *Burnham*, 68; *Cossack*,
46, 47; *Derwent*, 68, 74, 75; *Duncan*,
30, 56; *Eclipse*, 106; *Electra*, 39;
Encounter, 48; *Eridge*, 45; *Eskimo*,
25, 85, 98, 106, 108; *Fantasque* (Fr),
112; *Faulknor*, 62; *Fearless*, 42, 43,
44; *Firedrake*, 44, 45; *Foresight*, 43,
75; *Foxhound*, 30; *Garland*, 56;
Gurkha, 61; *Heythrop*, 56; *Icarus*,
39, 62, 75; *Imogen*, 39; *Isaac Sweers*
(Neth), 57; *Ithuriel*, 85; *Keppel*, 67;
Laforey, 81, 106; *Legion*, 25;
Lightning, 46; *Lookout*, 81, 106;
Loyal, 106; *Maori*, 44, 46, 47;
Meteor, 119; *Myngs*, 147; *Norman*,
62; *Nubian*, 106; *Opportune*, 119;
Oribi, 56; *Panther*, 92; *Pathfinder*,
74, 75; *Penn*, 140; *Piorun* (Pol), 56,
106; *Porcupine*, 92; *Punjabi*, 67;

159